THE
STORY
OF THE
ROYAL
FAMILY

CLB 1887
First published in Canada 1987 by Collins Royal.
©1987 Colour Library Books Ltd., Guildford, Surrey, England.
Printed and bound in Hong Kong by Leefung-Asco Printers Ltd
All rights reserved.
ISBN 0 86283 520 8

THE
STORY
OF THE
ROYAL
FAMILY

Text by
Trevor Hall

COLLINS
ROYAL

'If I am asked today,' said the Queen on her Silver Wedding anniversary, 'what I think about family life after twenty-five years of marriage, I can answer with simplicity and conviction: I am for it.'

We are always being told how important the family is in our society. Bishops praise it, government social policies are based on it, and charities seeking funds for the unloved point out how lucky most of us are to be members of a close-knit, caring family. The concept, like most, attracts its cynics, but in our heart of hearts we accept that there is nothing quite like the family when we need a point of reference, an anchor, a finger-post to cope with the confusions that sometime assail our entrenched, often servile attitudes to life, its meaning and the way it should be lived.

In that light it is hardly surprising that it is to a family – the Royal Family – that we should look in the wider context of our national identity, honour, pride – call it what you will. At the same time it seems quaintly eccentric, even pernicious to some, that a collection of individuals, born to their position by nothing more deserving than the whim of fortune, and said repeatedly in their defence to be as human as the rest of us, should be identified with power and influence in high places and enjoy privileges that would be the envy of millions.

It's a conundrum you can mull over for ever without really resolving. We know the hereditary principle is illogical in what we choose to label an egalitarian age. When things are going badly we resent the benefit that system confers on the Royal Family; we begrudge them their prerogatives, wince at the bowing and scraping, and deplore the expenditure of huge amounts of time and money desperately needed elsewhere. Yet, come a royal celebration or national rejoicing, we allow ourselves the luxury of absorbing the idea of a family up there presiding over our national affairs as not such a bad one after all. And there's nothing quite like the twinkle of tiaras, the jingle of the ceremonial horses' tack, the bray of trumpets and the sonorous boom of cannon in a distant park to convince us. It still doesn't make sense. It may be sheer, unthinking escapism. But it's there.

Like her grandfather King George V, and her great-great grandmother Queen Victoria, the Queen has a marked taste and affection for anniversaries and the memories they evoke. It is evident in countless of her speeches. Often, these memories involve other members of her family – if for no other reason than that many of her duties are elements of an annual royal round of which the family past and present has always been part, from the Braemar Games in Scotland, for instance, to Trooping the Colour and the Festival of Remembrance. For a century and a quarter it has been dispersed to all parts of the world for hundreds of royal visits. There are few places left for the Queen to go and not discover that one or other Royal Highness has beaten her to it.

The Queen may thus be forgiven if, in the year of her sixtieth birthday, she indulges not only in a few family memories, but also in the satisfying thought that both she and her royal relatives have done well to preserve and strengthen their position as the family unit to which we still cannot avoid turning, despite the passing of a generation of years that have been uncertain of direction, tumultuous in events, and sometimes depressing in outlook. If you have ever marvelled at how well the Royal Family – and the institution of monarchy which it serves – has come out of successive controversies and the difficulties which faced it as public attitudes towards it began to change, hindsight will already have shown that it was the concept of the family – rather than of a single monarchical figure, or of a faceless Constitution – that enabled that change in attitude to be encountered and absorbed.

When the Queen came to the throne in 1952, her family image may have seemed less significant, possibly because it was taken more for granted. Looking back, the Royal Family of post-War Britain seems a staid and over-respectable assortment of individuals, ultra-conservative in outlook, appearance, opinions and behaviour. The austerity from which the country was then only just emerging, and the profusion of monochrome newspaper, magazine and television photography in that twilight era of popular illustration in black-and-white only, lends an illusion of colourlessness to the image when compared with the dazzling effect of the high-quality colour reproduction available today.

Accordingly, the Queen's first achievement was a relatively effortless one – simply that of being a young, vivacious sovereign, set upon the throne in what were then seen as appallingly unexpected circumstances – the premature death of her father, George VI – which compounded the accident of history fifteen years earlier, when her uncle Edward VIII had abdicated 'for the woman I love'.

'Glamour' was hardly a respectable term in those days – too easily linked with the brash, glitzy world of the silver screen – but, for the public's money, Elizabeth II had all the outward appeal of a Hollywood film-star. With her fine features, lively eye and gleaming smile, she moved in august circles and in the prime of womanhood, exhibiting an impeccable gift for combining popular fashion with the need to dress for the occasion, the poise that comes of years of grooming for the part, modesty in abundance and charm to spare. Add to that a debonair husband who had for five years been the golden boy of the Royal Family, a pigeon pair of delightful children – Charles, serious at three years old, Anne a mischievous toddler – and a doting, indulgent grandmother, widowed at barely fifty years of age, and the picture was complete.

Few could resist marvelling at the comparisons with the young Queen Victoria, the experience of whose long and prosperous reign surely foretold of similar triumphs to come. Somehow this young, vulnerable family seemed to exude the promise of a glorious new Elizabethan age – in which context the death of that magnificent, archetypal Victorian, Queen Mary, just six weeks before Elizabeth's coronation, may have appeared more than symbolic. As we now know, and as the British public learned the hard way, new Elizabethan ages do not arrive merely by being proclaimed. The convictions that came of national wishful thinking in 1953 have been constantly assaulted by Cyprus and Suez, oil crises and economic decline, super-powerdom and terrorism, and the ceaseless, sometimes violent and hard-won struggle for social change.

It was indeed folly to be wise in those early days. The Coronation, for all the economies asked for by the Duke of Edinburgh when he chaired the first meeting of the Coronation Committee, was an extravaganza of a brilliance and on a scale unequalled in living memory. Implicit in its endless gold and silver trappings, its scarlets and purples, its ermines and embroideries, its ancient symbols of kingship and their veiled meanings, was a celebration not only of the best of Britain's colourful heritage, but also a statement of belief in its power to see Britain through any of her national difficulties.

The belief was shared by virtually everyone in that heady Coronation atmosphere, primarily because the entire event was seen on television, and was thus, for the first time, within the witness of a huge proportion of the Queen's admiring subjects. That was made possible thanks only to the Queen herself, for it was she who overruled her Prime Minister, Archbishop of Canterbury and Earl Marshal at a stroke when they advised against allowing the cameras in. It was a perfect example of the monarchy's skilful use of the media for what was effectively publicity purposes. The role of the Crown in history, the relevance of its traditions to its present-day activities, and the function of the monarchy within a democratic society were made visible and explicit against a glorious and memorable backdrop of ancient ceremonial. Its effect on the faithful in Christ was no less salutary. 'The United Kingdom last Tuesday,' said the Archbishop of Canterbury, 'was not very far from the Kingdom of Heaven.' And both the moving homage paid to the young sovereign by her husband, and the appearance of the four-year-old Prince Charles, brought to Westminster Abbey half way through the ceremony to join his aunt and grandmother as they watched from the Royal Gallery, served as reminders that it was not just the Queen, but her family, who were being presented and acclaimed on that day.

A few years of general public goodwill followed, based on that family vision. Everyone, for instance, seemed to share what was widely identified as the poignancy of the royal parents' departure for a six-month Commonwealth tour, involving as it did the necessity of leaving behind two young and impressionable children who had presumably seen precious little of their busy, pre-occupied mother and father in the previous couple of years. During the tour, the nation received, with the oohs and aahs of genuine affection, some officially released photographs showing the two temporary orphans enjoying a weekend with their grandmother at Royal Lodge, her Windsor retreat. And, towards its end, the family reunion – off Tobruk, during the royal visit to Libya – was relished nationally, even internationally, with vicarious emotion and pleasure.

Later there was the enormous interest – indeed thrill – of watching the heir to the Throne attending school in the heart of London, following his parents' decision to send him to public schools in preference to having him educated solely within the walls of Buckingham Palace. There were those delightful incidents during Royal Windsor Horse Shows, Badminton Horse Trials, or Windsor and Cowdray Park polo matches, when the whole family of four could be seen at least in a semblance of relaxation (for it paid, then as now, to be on your guard whenever the press was around): the Queen of England treading down the divots; her husband swinging his polo mallet as if his life depended on it; her children feeding ponies or buying mementoes at side-stalls; all four, plus Grannie and the aunts, uncles and cousins, spread out on rugs and blankets, well wrapped up against Gloucestershire's spring breezes and with only a picket fence separating them from the common herd, all watching horses being put through their paces. It was an idyllic national reverie, and with the profusion of new, colourful magazines and books to record it all, it was rarely other than hot news.

Like most dreams, this one eventually broke. Nineteen-fifty-five had been a disastrous year, ending as it did in the bitter moral confusion following Princess Margaret's renunciation of her suitor of many years, Group-Captain Peter Townsend. Townsend, a former equerry of the Princess' father before being transferred to the household of Queen Elizabeth the Queen Mother, was divorced, and in the high moral and religious atmosphere of the new Elizabethan age, royalty did not marry divorcees. The twenty years since the Abdication had not changed that.

Following a two-year-old simmering of speculation and innuendo in the British press (for the possibility of trouble had been publicly spotted as early as 1953), the story alleging an impending marriage burst into the papers and continued to maintain an unhealthy grip on their readers for six long and distressing months. Scenting, in that prolonged period of official silence, that royalty was on the run, the press became (for those days) openly impertinent, and the headline 'Come on, Margaret: Make up your mind' encapsulated the mood for posterity. Eventually, the Princess was obliged to issue a statement confirming her decision, 'mindful of the Church's teaching that Christian marriage is indissoluble, and conscious of my duty towards the Commonwealth,' not to marry her suitor. Townsend went quietly away to begin a new life.

For the Queen the whole affair was fraught with danger and the threat of dissention and obsessive sensation. She knew that from the beginning, of course, yet tackled it with remarkable calmness and personal sympathy for both her sister and the Group Captain which belied the disturbing possibilities of the case and the anxiety she must have felt. She at first refused to have Townsend banished from the Court – a suggestion put forward by both her Private Secretary and the Prime Minister – then, when her hand was forced at the height of the initial furore, defiantly selected him as her official Equerry-in-Waiting, and was seen chatting freely and amicably to him in public during an official tour of Northern Ireland.

Ultimately she had no constitutional alternative, as Head of the Church of England, to registering and insisting on her formal disapproval of the marriage. Yet it says much for her tact and sense of proportion that the two sisters were then, and have since been, close and appreciative of each other – in spite of the raised eyebrows when Princess Margaret later married Antony Armstrong-Jones, the constant public fixation with the state of that marriage, the distress of the eventual separation and divorce, and the perpetual, intransigent rumours that have dogged the Princess and reflected so badly on the Royal Family since.

As at the Abdication, the public was divided on the rights and wrongs of the Townsend affair, and although it died a decent death as 1956 came round, it soon became apparent that the issues and their treatment in the press had opened up the first questionings of the style of leadership which the Royal Family was adopting. People began to refer in disgruntled fashion to 'the Court' as the element to be criticised for its enduring resistance to change, its outmoded moral and social attitudes, and the consequent aloofness which threatened to alienate the Queen from her subjects. No-one was quite sure who 'the Court' was, but it afforded an acceptable alternative to direct criticism of the sovereign herself – a phenomenon unheard of since the days of Queen Victoria's prolonged mourning back in the 1870s. So without appearing to be disloyal or treasonable – indeed, with every appearance of being thoroughly loyal and protective towards the Queen personally – her critics could assail her advisers for their influences on her, the endless throng of titled hangers-on for sapping the Crown's privileges, and the continuing connection with the faded world of aristocrats (of which the annual presentation of debutantes provided the most glaring example) which had long since ceased to hold the country in thrall.

No sooner had that convenient avenue of hostility been explored than the Queen herself came in for a spate of criticism unparalleled either before or since. Her own childhood awareness of her future role in life had left her with a natural resistance to change and with many of the rather more unfortunate accomplishments of standard royal behaviour which by 1957 was becoming more famous for its anachronistic courtliness than for its relevance to either present or future. In that year, Lord Altrincham vented a sudden and pronounced condemnation of the Queen's personal style in which he described 'the personality conveyed by the utterances put into her mouth' as 'that of a priggish schoolgirl.' The playwright John Osborne had already likened the monarchy to 'the gold filling in the mouth of decay' and had questioned the political value, social relevance and moral stimulus of 'the royal round of gracious boredom, the protocol of ancient fatuity.' As the new editor of *Punch*, Malcolm Muggeridge summarily discontinued that magazine's whimsical and unctuous support of the monarchy as an institution and of the Royal Family as individuals, made his own personal complaints about the Queen's 'dowdy, frumpish' appearance and 'banal' behaviour, deplored the cult of monarchy that had swept the country in the previous ten years and likened its mystical and traditional ceremonies to 'aspirins for a sick society. As a religion, monarchy has always been a failure. A God-King inevitably gets eaten.'

Before 1957 was out, it had become more personal than that. Late the previous year, the Duke of Edinburgh had left Britain for a four-month Commonwealth tour. Not for the first time, he was absent from his wife on their wedding anniversary, and although the Queen took their enforced separation as a theme of her Christmas message – 'My husband's absence at this time has made me even more aware than I was before of my own good fortune in being one of a united family....' – the press began to circulate the tale that not all was well with the royal marriage. Everything from the Duke's repeated absences, to disagreements about the children's education or the organisation of Palace staff was dragged in to support the growing speculation, and a handful of so-called eye-witness accounts from within the Palace – including one which alleged that the Duke had flung a sheaf of papers to his office floor in exasperation after a fruitless conversation with his wife – were cobbled together in an effort to prove it.

Few sensations of this nature have ever lasted long, and a springtime State Visit to Portugal that year seemed tailor-made for at least the appearance of a reconciliation. The Duke travelled to Lisbon direct from Gibraltar, the last port of call of his tour, while the Queen arrived direct from London. The couple were afforded forty minutes' 'private conversation time' inside the Queen's aircraft. As they emerged, one hawk-eyed reporter swore he spotted a little patch of lipstick on the Duke's left cheek, and everyone noticed he was wearing a tie with tiny hearts on it. What better proof could anybody want that the royal rift had been healed? And as if to consolidate the fact, the Queen created her husband a Prince of the United Kingdom – just a hundred years after Queen Victoria created *her* husband Prince Consort.

But the cumulative experience of two difficult years was not lost on the Queen, nor upon the Duke, who was now being credited with making the first steps to 'modernise' the monarchy. By the end of 1958, the debutante presentation parties had ceased in favour of the now famous royal garden parties, to which guests are selected on an immeasurably wider basis. The royal couple began to give monthly Palace luncheons for small groups of public figures – again representing a broad range of activities, from politics to sport and the arts. And the beginnings of greater public exposure occurred with the televising of the Queen's Christmas broadcasts, an illustrated television lecture given by the Duke on his 1956-7 tour, his first BBC interview, and ultimately the televising of State and ceremonial occasions, like Trooping the Colour and the State Opening of Parliament. In her first televised broadcast, the Queen had said, 'It is inevitable that I should seem a rather remote figure to many of you – a successor to the kings and queens of history', but the very occasion showed the flaw in her premise. If there was a feeling of isolation between ruler and ruled, it was no longer inevitable. The Queen's active achievement in bringing the Crown to her subjects dates from this time.

She was undoubtedly helped by the continuous, indeed prodigious family activity which brought the entire institution back into focus and favour after 1959. In August of that year the Queen announced that she was expecting her third child – after a gap of over nine years. The universal surprise at this news, coming at the end of a lengthy trip to Canada in which her health had caused anxiety and spawned mysterious and unsatisfactory official explanations, the fact that this would be the first child born to her as Queen, and the reflection that no baby had been born to a reigning sovereign since Queen Victoria's youngest, Princess Beatrice, over a century before, combined to make the Queen something of a heroine. There was a monumental outburst of patriotism around the Palace gates as her confinement approached, and the eventual news of the birth of a prince gladdened a cold and bleak February. Within the next week, two further events kept the Royal Family in the forefront of public attention – the death of Lady Edwina Mountbatten, and, more significantly, the engagement of Princess Margaret to Antony Armstrong-Jones.

Antony Armstrong-Jones had been a 'society' photographer, appointed by the Royal Family to take official photographs of them for the previous four years or so. His ability to recreate the formality of the Victorian royal photograph (as with the Queen's tenth wedding anniversary pictures in 1957), yet blend dignity with the occasional hint of informality (as with the portraits of Prince Charles and Princess Anne the same year) helped to edge the image of the Queen's immediate family away from the rather fulsome studio effects created by Marcus Adams in earlier decades. He had also taken many of Princess Margaret's birthday portraits during those years, and photographer and sitter had formed a strong, lasting relationship which existed entirely within the privacy of their own, vaguely avant-garde circle. That the announcement, and the Princess' choice of husband, caught the gossip-columnists of the national and international press completely unawares was a tribute to the discretion maintained by the couple's many close friends and associates.

At the same time the engagement did wonders for the process of undoing the Royal Family's remoteness, which the Queen had spoken of back in 1957. Though the genealogists rummaged through their books to discover the bridegroom's royal connections (like his fiancée, he was 23rd in descent from Edward I), there was something rather liberating about the fact that essentially this was a man of commoner origins, without even the shadow of a title in his close ancestry to justify his marriage in the eyes of the diehards. Establishment eyebrows may well have been raised as the guest list was prepared to show a large number of the couple's 'bohemian' friends, noses turned up at wild suggestions that they would start their married life in a flat in Pimlico, and mouths dropped at the realisation that because *his* father had married three times, *she* would have three mothers-in-law. But the truth was that when, on returning into the body of Westminster Abbey after signing the registers, the Princess was described as Mrs Antony Armstrong-Jones, the Royal Family moved a good step closer to every other family in the land.

It was perverse that, when the novelty had worn off, the groom should have been criticised for sponging off the Royal Family and enjoying privileges that most commoners never come within spitting distance of. A costly honeymoon cruise on the *Britannia*, an expensive refurbishment and repair programme to their Kensington Palace apartment, and a place at high table for every State occasion that he could be present at, were all catalysts for the critics. Yet, when he eventually took a permanent job at the Design Centre, then with the *Sunday Times*, he was again taken to task for demeaning the image of his in-laws. His one saving grace was that he did not take a title upon his marriage. That made him very much 'one of us' – until in October 1961, with the birth of his first child only a month away, the Queen bestowed the Earldom of Snowdon upon him. Whether this came at the

Queen's suggestion, or at the new Earl's request, or – as was commonly thought – at the insistence of Princess Margaret because she could not bear to see her children living untitled lives – was never made clear, and perhaps never will be. But it blew part of the legend for ever.

In the meantime the marriage of British royalty with commoners became itself more commonplace. In 1961, the Duke of Kent married Miss Katharine Worsley, the daughter of a North Yorkshire baronet, and two years later the Duke's sister, Princess Alexandra married the Hon Angus Ogilvy, the second son of the Earl of Airlie. And with all three marriages came a spate of royal children. After Prince Andrew's birth in 1960 and that of Viscount Linley the following year, came the birth of the Kents' first child – George, Earl of St Andrews – in 1962. Two years later all four young royal mothers produced children within two months of one another. Princess Alexandra's son James came first (on Leap Year's Day), the Queen's third son, Prince Edward, followed ten days later; then the Duchess of Kent's daughter, Lady Helen Windsor, arrived at the end of April, three days before Princess Margaret's daughter, Lady Sarah Armstrong-Jones, on May Day. The Year of the Royal Babies, as it became known, was the climax of a four-year period that saw the number of royal children of Prince Charles' generation increase from two to nine (eleven if you count two others born out of wedlock to the Harewood brothers – but that's another story).

It also saw the end of another period of intense interest in, and immense popularity for, the Royal Family. Three years passed by which were relatively quiet in terms of publicity, highlighted only by such events as the State Funeral of Sir Winston Churchill, the Queen's first State Visit to West Germany, the launching of the *QEII* and some lengthy Commonwealth tours. It was during this comparatively low-profile period that the Queen addressed herself to one particularly delicate family matter. For over thirty years the Duke and Duchess of Windsor had been virtual outcasts of the family whose name they bore. Since the Duke's voluntary exile in 1936, he and his wife had been infrequent and irregular visitors to Britain, prompted to return here only by urgent family and national matters – the outbreak of War in 1939, a meeting with Queen Mary in 1945, the funeral of King George VI in 1952, and so on.

In 1965, the Duke and Duchess came to London where the Duke underwent medical treatment to one of his eyes. The Queen took the opportunity to call in on him at his hotel, Claridge's, and spend an hour or so talking with both him and the Duchess. It was a private meeting, but publicly acknowledged, and it created great speculation that the Abdication, its cause and effect, would all be forgiven if not forgotten. It certainly looked as if the frequent public outcries against the Royal Family's apparent indifference or incivility towards the Windsors was having an effect, and that this visit was the Queen's way of showing that private relations between them were not as bad as everyone seemed to think.

Two years later the Windsors were back in London again, this time by virtue of a royal invitation to a public ceremony. Nineteen-sixty-seven was the centenary year of the birth of Queen Mary, and her grand-daughter was to unveil a plaque to her memory in the wall of Marlborough House, the old Queen's London residence for the last eight years of her life. It would indeed have been churlish and unforgiveable if the Duke had not been invited to attend the unveiling, but few people might have expected the invitation to extend to the Duchess. Queen Mary herself was implacably opposed to the former Mrs Simpson, and right up to her death could bring herself to no point of reconciliation beyond that of adding a postscript to one of her letters to her son which read, 'I send a kind message to your wife.' It was and is strongly believed that Queen Elizabeth the Queen Mother was at least as firmly opposed to the Duchess of Windsor's being received at Court or accorded any treatment implying her acceptance into the family. But other contemporaries, notably the then Duke and Duchess of Gloucester and Princess Marina, had visited the Windsors in the past, while the younger generation in the persons of Prince Charles and Princess Alexandra had more recently paid their respects when in Paris. The Queen clearly decided that her most senior aunt's continued exclusion from the family could no longer be justified, and that she should therefore be invited to join the Duke at Marlborough House. Which she did, thus ending in full public view a spiritual as well as physical exile which had lasted three decades. She was then in her seventy-first year.

Five years later, the Queen was in Paris on her second State Visit to France. At short notice, and much to the interest of royal-watchers on both sides of the Channel, a brief visit to the Windsors' house in the Bois de Boulogne was included in the royal schedule. The undisclosed reason for this late change to a programme agreed weeks before spawned widespread speculation. More gratuitous goodwill on both sides? Another public display of reconciliation? The chance of a home for the Windsors in Britain? The Duchess to become Her Royal Highness as last? A hint of the answer came with the news that the Duke was not well enough to greet his niece, and could meet her only in his room. After the meeting, only the Duchess came outside to see the Queen, Prince Philip and Prince Charles leave. The royal smiles, and even the Duchess' pained, fixed pursing of the lips hid for the moment the fact that the Duke's days were numbered. He would lie on his death-bed for no more than eight more days before finally succumbing to advanced cancer of the throat.

Apart from the Duchess' brief stay at Buckingham Palace for the Duke's obsequies, there seemed no reconciliation even in death. The body of the former monarch was interred at Frogmore after lying-in-State at Windsor, all in accordance with his wishes. His widow, who directly afterwards left Britain unescorted by any member of her dead husband's family, still found no home in his native country. Only when, in her 90th year, her distressing, prolonged and weary senility finally ended, did she return to lie beside him for ever in that peaceful and very royal corner of England.

This long-running royal controversy may well have seemed a world away from the bright promise which the younger generation of the Royal Family offered back in 1967. In that year Prince Charles completed his five-year secondary education at Gordonstoun, the Scotland-based school which his father had attended and to which both his brothers were to follow him, and went up to Cambridge to begin a three-year degree course in history, archaeology and anthropology. The choice of these heavily academic subjects disappointed many people for whom they implied that the student himself would be a dull, possibly pedantic plodder. In a sense, that reaction proved how little was known about him at the time, and thus how well the Queen had managed to keep her son out of the public eye since he first trotted off to school in 1957.

It was not long before the Prince showed his true colours. From the modest, reserved boy he had always seemed to be, he emerged, long before the end of his first year at Cambridge, as a sensible, thoughtful student with a personable nature and a refreshing, slightly zany, sense of humour. The popular suspicions that, for all the Queen's attempts to bring him up as normally as possible, he would turn out as a ready-made king-to-be, processed out of Establishment material from the inner sanctums of Buckingham Palace, were quickly dispelled as he threw himself into the University's social, as well as academic, life. It was at Cambridge that he developed his musical talents, learning to play the trumpet (until one of his orchestral colleagues couldn't stand the sound he was making), and subsequently taking up the cello. He became an active member of the University's Dryden Dramatic Society, and was soon famous as a man of many parts, playing the roles of dustmen, vicars, lechers and spoilt aristocrats with equal adroitness, displaying his long-standing and recently disclosed affection for the crazy humour of the Goons, and, most important of all, able and willing to allow some of his audience's laughter to be turned against himself. 'Were it not for my ability to see the funny side of my life,' he once said, 'I'd have been committed to an institution long ago.'

As it happened, the emergence of this side of the Prince's character, its relative openness, frankness and – despite his having been brought up very much in the company of older people – refreshing youthfulness, provided the impetus for the next stage in the monarchy's move towards closer identification with its subjects. Back in 1958, the Queen had created her son Prince of Wales and promised to present him to the Welsh people at Caernarfon 'when he is grown up.' A decade later she decided that 1969 would be the year in which this ceremonial presentation would be acted out, and in the year-long run-up to the event she approved a monumental publicity exercise (not to put too fine a point on it) which broke so many shackles with the restrictive practices of the past that to all public appearances the Royal Family has never been the same since.

By and large, the idea was to drive home the fact that the Queen and her growing family were, at heart, no more than human, like everybody else. To put the idea across, she authorised the production of a blockbusting television film documentary, called simply *Royal Family*, in which the cameras were allowed to film the Queen and her relations at work and at play. The Queen was seen in her office at Buckingham Palace, scrutinising draft speeches, choosing jewellery for the next State Visit, and approving a new set of postage stamps; Prince Philip was shown discussing with his staff the logistics of travel in order to squeeze as many engagements into a day as possible, then climbing into a helicopter in the grounds of the Palace; Prince Charles was seen bicycling round Cambridge, shopping for provisions, and making shift for himself in his rooms; Princess Anne was filmed during a lesson at the Berlitz School of Languages where she was undergoing a course in French. Of the younger children, Prince Andrew was playing football at his school in Berkshire, while Prince Edward, then only five, shared a lesson in the Buckingham Palace schoolroom with his cousins and close friends.

On the purely official side there were inside shots for the very first time of a royal Investiture, and of the Queen giving numerous audiences to ambassadors, High Commissioners, foreign heads of state (including President Nixon), and heads of Commonwealth governments. She was seen hosting a Buckingham Palace garden party, the annual Diplomatic Reception, and a less formal, but no less well-attended, Palace reception for the British Olympic team, and carrying out her outside duties in Britain and during her 1968 State Visit to South America. It was a fascinating (if, for obvious reasons, not totally complete) insight into the workings of monarchy, and brought home the fact that an enormous amount of hard graft and thought behind the scenes goes into the work of a sovereign, which most people see as only a superficial, rather easy job where everything runs smoothly and predictably.

But most important of all, the film achieved its main objective of projecting the Royal Family as a family of individuals with the attributes (if not the lifestyle) of ordinary human beings. It disproved the falsehoods that they never eat together, or that they never do anything for themselves, or that they have equerries and ladies-in-waiting around them wherever they go. Here was film of Prince Charles whizzing around a Windsor Castle courtyard in a go-kart, of Prince Edward being rowed across a Scottish lake by his father, of Prince Andrew snowballing with his younger brother at Sandringham, of Prince Philip painting a water-colour at Windsor. Here was the whole family enjoying a barbecue on the Balmoral estate, with the Queen helping Prince Charles to mix the salad dressing, the Duke and Princess Anne grilling sausages and steaks. Here they were chatting casually at the lunch table at Buckingham Palace, swopping stories about everything from King George VI's temper to hilarious incidents during state visits. Here was the Queen and Prince Philip travelling by air from one engagement to another – *he* putting the finishing touches to a speech, *she* reading *The Sporting Life* to keep up with the latest racing developments. And here was the whole family – sisters, cousins and aunts – sharing Christmas at Windsor; the Queen's four children helping to dress a huge Christmas tree, the Snowdons' children picking out their favourite ancestral portraits under the benign eye of the Queen Mother, the young Kent cousins all dressed up in smart white woollies and bobble hats, ready for outdoor games, and the Ogilvy children ploughing down the corridors in their toy cars, followed by Princess Alexandra pushing a trolley laden with presents.

And so it went on. The film, shown only days before Prince Charles' Investiture, was rapturously received, watched by almost 75% of Britain's population, and clamoured for by the rest of the Western world. It made the Investiture itself – a modernised ceremony, yet packed full of ancient ritual and sonority – somehow surprisingly relevant, where otherwise it may have seemed a mere dressing-up charade with king, queen, jacks, jokers and all. And without doubt it ushered in the new royal generation, and paved the way for the style its young representatives would adopt if the monarchy were to be made as relevant to the 21st century as it had been in the twentieth.

Setting the pace for this renaissance were Prince Charles himself and his sister Princess Anne. The Prince continued to busy himself at Cambridge, which he left with a History degree in 1970 to take up a naval career for the following six years. In that time he combined his service duties with a wide range of official programmes, dispensing independence to various Commonwealth countries, representing the Queen at foreign coronations and the funerals of heads of state, and touring the world both with and without his parents. In those kinds of capacities he was seen far and wide, in a variety of new, colourful and appealing locations, trying his hand at a whole range of new experiences. And unlike his mother before him, he felt able – possibly obliged – to take part actively in whatever amusement or diversion was offered to him. The Queen would never climb a ladder, wield a snooker cue, pick up a child, dive into a crowd, or press any button unless the consequence was absolutely guaranteed. Prince Charles, even in those early years, seemed irresistibly drawn to that very kind of behaviour. He crawled into igloos, walked upside-down on the underside of Arctic ice, rode camels, performed love-dances in Fiji, dressed up in Ghanaian tribal chiefs' robes, smoked peace-pipes in Canada, and was more than once on the receiving end of custard pies.

Princess Anne undertook her first solo engagement at the age of eighteen, and lost no time in making her own impact on a curious and receptive public. Her two strengths were her flair for colourful clothes and penchant for eye-catching hats, and her forthright manner which, at the occasional risk of appearing brusque, reminded everyone much more of her father than of her mother. In the four years before her marriage, her impressive wardrobe of clothes made her by far the most talked-about and sought-after member of the Royal Family. She made a point of buying British, choosing frequently off the peg, and patronising the departmental stores rather than the standard Palace couturiers and fashion houses. In her choice of day clothes she took fullest advantage of the trend towards stunning, vivid colours, and appeared in emerald greens, peacock blues, shocking pinks, tomato reds and sunshine yellows with a regularity and predictability that made her a standard target for any press photographer wishing to stay in work. Her evening dresses were little short of magnificent: with her mature eye for style with dignity, her love of shimmering colour, and her dazzling collection of personal jewellery, she outshone all around her to such a degree that she was frequently accused of having upstaged the Queen herself. She often denied that she had any appreciable eye for fashion, shrugged off the 'swinging princess' label that had been tagged onto her, and even once protested that she thought herself rather staid. But her wide-brimmed hats, trouser-suits, mini-skirts and squat-heeled shoes echoed the burgeoning youthfulness of the times and may have done more than anyone realised to maintain that ethereal relationship between Crown and people that, rightly or wrongly, depends these days as much upon surface trivia as upon deep-rooted respect for tradition and matriarchy.

If the delicacy of that relationship was ever in doubt, it was illustrated by Princess Anne's other quality – the honesty of approach and reaction that suffers no fool gladly, and (to use phraseology of which she would approve) lets one know exactly where one stands. She once told the Americans that a bald eagle for their national symbol was 'a rather bad choice', insisted that she was delighted she never had a sister, condemned tennis as 'far too gladiatorial', complained that she would never get a good career, and warned all and sundry that 'I don't enjoy being pushed and shoved around by other people.' She has openly admitted not being 'much enamoured of London', and has condemned smokers, drinkers, people who make long speeches, and those who serve her exotic food. Her tirades against the press soon became as legendary as they were successively controversial. No Badminton or Burghley was complete in the early 1970s without a volley of protest from competitor HRH Princess Anne which usually ended with a choice phrase from her substantial armoury of maledictions. 'Go Away', 'Clear Out', 'Get Lost' and 'Shove Off' all became respectable through constant and well-reported royal usage.

In many ways, this honest and unbridled show of independence and self-respect rebounded upon her. 'Who learned Princess Anne to swear?' asked one five-year-old child once. The point was not lost on the Princess, who herself admitted that 'when I appear in public, people expect me to neigh, grind my teeth, paw the ground and swish my tail.' But her behaviour, and the courage she showed in exhibiting it, won her many admirers. Even her critics came eventually to see her side of a controversy which was often reported one-sidedly by her main victims, the press. 'You tend to be rather a touchy lot, too,' she chided them once, and they didn't disagree. What was more, she proved to be one of the first to give the lie to the belief that royalty cannot answer back. In many respects it still can't, but there are limits even to royal patience at times, and these days you get no credit for reining in your tongue when to do the opposite would be everyone else's natural reaction.

Ever since her official launching onto the public scene, Princess Anne had been carefully watched by the press and public for signs that she would marry. The opportunities for speculation were very limited. Her sole recreational interest appeared to be in the horse world and, as she herself admitted, never with the sophisticated night-club life that had so attracted her aunt Princess Margaret and her great uncle Edward VIII. And her equestrian involvement was total and uncompromising, a constant and progressive effort that stopped at nothing short of the excellence that eventually won her the European Championship in 1971. It seemed that her frequent and unconcealed meetings and conversations with male companions from the world of eventing and show-jumping – notably Richard Meade and Andrew Parker-Bowles – were too obvious to carry romantic connotations, and it was consequently a long time before the companionship of one Lieut. Mark Phillips was seized upon by the press as being anything other than platonic. By the end of 1972, Lieut. Phillips had proved himself an excellent horseman, with two Badminton championships to his credit and a clutch of honours from his participation in British teams for successive European, Olympic and World Championships.

He had also proved himself to be a prime contender for the hand of the Queen's daughter, the public assumption of which was strengthened by the many sightings the following spring of the Princess and the Lieutenant training and exercising their horses together in preparation for the eventing season to come. More than once they faced a bevy of photographers in the middle of these training sessions, and more than once Princess Anne issued her authoritative and quick-tempered denials that there was anything more between them than a love of horses. Only after the 1973 Badminton – in which Princess Anne finished eighth and Mark finished up in the lake – did the tone of her responses soften and their appearances together become more circumspectly arranged. By the end of May they were engaged. By the end of the year they were married.

The marriage of members of the Royal Family, particularly where romance has been long suspected and denied, is often followed by a falling off of public interest, as if each wedding were the culmination of a particular story. To an extent this was true of Princess Anne, though their claim to popular attention was momentarily revived early in 1974 after a gunman tried to kidnap her, and the following year when Gatcombe Park was purchased for her and her husband by the Queen. Certainly Prince Philip had been aware of how easily established members of the Royal Family can be lost sight of. Back in the 1960s he admitted that he and the Queen were entering a stage of life at which the glamour has worn off – and he was right. With popular interest focused strongly on their two elder children, the Queen and her husband spent much of the 1970s in comparative shade, maintaining a regular and conscientious work schedule that only rarely produced anything totally new or spectacular.

There was no conscious effort to counter this inevitable shift in popularity, and it would have been wrong for it to be otherwise. Nevertheless. one of the main highlights of the decade was centred upon the Queen and Prince Philip, not only as individuals, but also as the senior members of a nation's surrogate family. This was very much a family affair – the Silver Wedding celebrations in November 1972, marked by a thanksgiving service in Westminster Abbey and a Lord Mayoral luncheon at the Guildhall. It was at this luncheon that the Queen reaffirmed her personal commitment to the sanctity of the family unit, speaking of the relationship between man and wife as capable of maturity and development only if it is 'held firm in the web of family relationships between parents and children, grandparents and grandchildren, cousins, aunts and uncles.'

To commemorate the event for posterity, and almost as if to reinforce the Queen's sentiments, the royal couple had a wealth of photographs officially released, many of which were taken at and around Balmoral during the previous summer holidays. Some of these pictures depicted all four of their children, as indeed did a later portfolio of photographs, taken on the wedding anniversary itself, in which congratulatory telegrams were being opened and relished.

But more significant for the perpetuation of that all-important family image was the set of pictures taken by the Queen Mother's nephew, Lord Lichfield, in which most of the surviving representatives of the families of King George V's children were shown. With the Queen's immediate family were the Queen Mother, Princess Margaret and Lord Snowdon with their children, the Duke and Duchess of Kent with theirs (including the two-year-old Lord Nicholas Windsor), the bachelor Prince Michael, and Princess Alexandra and her family. Only the Harewoods, the two sons of the late Princess Royal, were missing, presumably by reason of their untoward history of extra-marital relationships, and the Gloucesters, for whom the early 1970s was a particularly tragic time.

Despite its comparative seniority, the Gloucester family has always preferred to exist in the shadows of publicity. By nature a shy man, the old Duke of Gloucester was a dutiful and reliable, if unimaginative, royal who enjoyed nothing better than the straightforward private life of a securely-based aristocrat. Country pleasures and the company of tried and trusted friends were all he asked, and in this he found a perfect companion in his wife. They had two children, though quite late in life, and at the temporary expense of the Duchess' health and several miscarriages. In 1967 the Duke suffered a stroke which left him badly paralysed and virtually speechless. His wife took on a large proportion of the duties in respect of which he was in receipt of Civil List payments, and their elder son Prince William was made aware that his chosen diplomatic career would have to come to an end rather sooner that had otherwise been expected.

By that frustrating irony which afflicts the Royal Family as much as anyone, it was Prince William who died first. A fanatic for speed and adventure, he entered himself for an air race at Wolverhampton in August, 1972. His plane had hardly left the ground before it turned, banked steeply, lost height and crashed to the ground in flames. The news of his instant death, brought to his seventy-year-old mother by another competitor, numbed her beyond grief. Coupled with the difficult and distressing anguish of caring for her invalid and virtually helpless husband during the two further years that preceded his death, the experience persuaded her that she should retire from public life altogether.

It says much for the Royal Family's sense of duty that she allowed her decision to be reversed. Her younger son, Prince Richard, and the Danish born Birgitte van Deurs whom he had married only seven weeks before Prince William died, took on full-time duties as the new Duke and Duchess of Gloucester, while the widowed Duchess, now known as Princess Alice, found it impossible to loose herself from the many enjoyable associations she had made during her forty years as a member of the Royal Family. At the time of her eightieth birthday, she resolved again to reduce the numbers of her public engagements, but again without success. 'The trouble is,' she explained, 'that when you have been associated with organisations for so many years, and they plead with you to do something again that you did for them last year, or say it's all going to be a terrible flop if you don't go, what can you do?'

And so, half-way through her eighties, she goes on. She is now the proud grandmother of three youngsters – Alexander, Earl of Ulster, born in 1974, and Ladies Davina and Rose Windsor, born in 1977 and 1980 respectively. She has certainly appreciated the truth of the Queen's perception of the importance of the family, as expressed in that Silver Wedding speech. Though, even as she spoke those words, the Queen herself must have been aware of the irony of her remarks. For at that very time the marriage of her sister, Princess Margaret, and Lord Snowdon was going through a traumatic stage of bitterness and indifference from which it was never to recover. The whys and wherefores of the growing estrangement, and the rights and wrongs of the case, are still the subject of debate and dispute, and blame has been variously apportioned ever since by all manner of people claiming to have been in the know. What is clear is that rumours of family rows, sudden absences and alleged affairs had been mounting steadily for several years and that Lord Snowdon was being seen less and less frequently in the company of his wife as the 1970s wore on. Thus the announcement, early in 1976, that the Princess and her husband were to separate came as no great surprise and, as if there were some kind of universal relief that the tension of so many years' speculation had been released at last, the couple were left to live out the two-year period before their inevitable divorce in relative peace and privacy. In 1978 the Princess obtained a dissolution of the marriage under what is glibly called the 'quickie' system, by which the High Court may grant an instant divorce on mutually agreed evidence that the parties have lived apart for two years and consider the breakdown of their marriage to be irreconcilable.

Conversely, and not without its own hint of irony, another royal romance was on the horizon, with not only divorce but also religion among its potential hazards. Prince Michael of Kent, whose elder brother and sister had each married in the early 1960s, had formed a tenacious and well-publicised attachment with the former Baroness Marie-Christine von Reibnitz, a Czech-born lady of aristocratic antecedents whose marriage to a Mr Thomas Troubridge had already effectively broken down. It was well-known by the beginning of 1978 (when Princess Margaret's marriage was nearing its own end) that Prince Michael was waiting only for the Troubridge union to be annulled before he could go to the Queen and request her consent to wed Marie-Christine. In the more liberated atmosphere of the times (the Earl of Harewood had remarried following his divorce in 1967, and his brother was about to follow suit), and with Prince Michael being sixteenth in the line of succession, the Queen's consent would not have been difficult to give, but the fact that the lady was a Roman Catholic posed constitutional problems which it was not within the Queen's power to ignore.

The outcome effectively relegated the ghost of the Abdication controversy, to which it was likened, to the history books. The Baroness' annulment proved no bar to the Queen's permission for the Prince to marry her, and any religious objection was overcome by the simple expedient of Prince Michael's renunciation of his purely academic right of succession. It was not much to give up for the prospect of a lifetime's happiness, particularly as the renunciation did not extend to the couple's children. Indeed, the circumstances of the romance (which culminated in a Viennese wedding in June, 1978) raised Marie-Christine almost embarrassingly high in public esteem. She proved more than worthy of the accolade. High-spirited, yet of regal bearing, cultivated, colourful and considerate, she seemed to require no instruction on how to walk with kings nor lose the common touch. Despite, possibly because of, the persistent journalistic knifings she suffered at the hands of one gossip columnist in particular, she has been immensely popular and her presence in public is highly sought after. Her long and determined battle to win Papal recognition for her second marriage was blessed with success after five years of effort and uncertainty, and she came through the appalling opprobrium which followed the revelation of her father's membership of the German SS during the War with a humility and dignity that begged no forgiveness yet won universal sympathy.

The major royal events of the late 1970s might well have suggested that the fierce glare of publicity had shifted back from the younger to the older generations of the Royal Family. The Queen's Silver Jubilee of 1977 was certainly another indication that in spite of the appeal of youth, a national sentiment and goodwill still existed in favour of those with a proven royal record – and in this of all years, the Queen was the epitome of reliability and accumulated wisdom. She had already reigned longer than two-thirds of her predecessors since the Norman Conquest, and although initially there was, in the adverse economic and social climate, little national appetite for a full-blown celebration of what was, after all, an anniversary of a purely arbitrary significance in time, the feeling gained momentum that throughout a quarter century of enormous, unprecedented and often bewildering change, the Queen remained the one constant factor. Older and staider she might be – certainly she had lost, gracefully and imperceptibly, the polished bloom and vivacity of her early womanhood – but she was as dedicated as ever, still smiling despite the little personal troubles, family problems and occasional constitutional storms which she had been obliged to weather.

And, of course, as the official celebrations confirmed, she had around her a huge family which, for all its diversity of age, seniority, interests and lifestyle, was probably more tightly united that most in Britain. Prince Philip was, at 55, still prolonging and extending his associations with such organisations as the World Wildlife Fund, the Duke of Edinburgh's Award Scheme and the Royal Yacht Squadron, and remained the Royal Family's mouthpiece on all manner of subjects regardless of their controversial implications. Prince Charles, then nearing thirty, had proved a good all-rounder, absorbing his experiences as heir to the throne more widely and deeply than any of his predecessors. Princess Anne, a 27-year-old mother-to-be, was acquiring a reputation as a committed and indefatigable worker for prime good causes such as the Save The Children Fund and the Riding for the Disabled Association. Prince Andrew was approaching his constitutional majority and a twelve-year career in the Royal Navy, while his younger brother, 14-year-old Prince Edward, remained very much an unknown quantity, enjoying a more complete degree of personal privacy than any of his siblings before him.

Beyond the Queen's immediate family, Princess Margaret pursued her royal duties with an emphasis on the arts, while her estranged husband busied himself with a host a photographic projects which took him all over the world. Their children were still at school – Bedales on the Hampshire/Sussex borders – and thus not yet within sight of the careers that would make a woodwork designer out of Viscount Linley, and Lady Sarah an art student. Then came the three generations of the Gloucesters, a quiet, dependable family devoted to its own thriving farming business in Northamptonshire when not on royal call; and finally the growing Kent clan.

The Duke and Duchess of Kent's three children grew apace: young George was at Eton, revelling in the beginnings of a brilliantly successful education that would eventually send him to Cambridge and earn him the reputation of being the brainiest member of the Royal Family; his sister Helen was already supporting the long-held theory that the females of the Kent family had, ever since Princess Marina married Prince George in 1934, been easily the most attractive of all in the Royal Family – though it was some years before birthday portraits by Lord Snowdon and Tim Graham would show her to be not only superbly photogenic but also quite exceptionally lovely.

George and Helen's younger brother Nicholas was seven years old in Jubilee year. Born over six years after his sister, he was considered very much a 'late addition' to the family, though in fact there was hope for an even later addition when the Duchess of Kent fell pregnant again in mid-1977. Unhappily, though perhaps not surprisingly, for she was then almost 45 years of age, she was rushed to hospital in late October where she suffered a miscarriage. Though she seemed to overcome the physical and psychological strains of that pregnancy and its outcome, the distress signalled a six-year period of health problems for the Duchess, whose chief attribute with her public was her deep, uninhibited, caring and very personal involvement with the handicapped, the sick and the dying. The successive health crises in her own life until 1983 brought her and her family into a prominence quite disproportionate to their position in the line of succession, as well as unsought by and distasteful to them personally.

The Ogilvies – the most junior-ranking branch of the Kent family - were luckier in their quest for the quiet life, which they successfully secured until threatened by the taint of scandal in the wake of the Lonrho affair during Jubilee year itself. Back in 1973, a series of allegations concerning the activities of some of the directors of the international company Lonrho – of which Mr Ogilvy was one – rocked the business world and even elicited the public condemnation of the Prime Minister, Edward Heath. Wisely, Mr Ogilvy resigned his directorship, along with fifty or so other similar posts which he had acquired long before his marriage to the Princess in 1963. By 1977, and in the belief of exoneration, he had begun to re-acquire directorships, but the story gained credence, against the hottest public denials, that criminal charges against him were being considered by the Director of Public Prosecutions. Any such prospective action came to nothing. Princess Alexandra continues now, as she did then, to fulfil the modest supporting role that has been hers since she reached the age of eighteen in 1954. Her husband, despite recurrent health problems affecting his back and his eyesight, maintains his City associations and his interest in art through his directorship of Sotheby's. Their children, James and Marina, aged 13 and nine respectively in Jubilee year, followed a quiet, uninterrupted lifestyle of which their cousins in Buckingham Palace might have been more than a little envious.

Though the Queen stood at the head of this expanding family, there were others around her whom she might well have considered not only older, but also wiser than she, and in many respects the following years – especially from 1979 to 1981 – were memorable in connection with them, and arguably with them alone. In August 1979 (almost on the very anniversaries of the death of Prince George, Duke of Kent on active service in 1942, and of Prince William of Gloucester in 1972), Lord Mountbatten was killed when the fishing boat he was sailing in was blown up by the IRA off the north-west coast of Ireland. In that split second, Prince Philip lost an uncle and surrogate father, the Queen lost a valued adviser, Prince Charles lost a mentor to whom he was unashamedly devoted, and the Royal Family lost a man who, for all his vanity and persistence on behalf of himself and the name of Mountbatten, was probably at the root of the triumph of survival and popularity in which the monarchy could at that very moment justifiably bask. He was in his eightieth year at the time of his deplorable murder, and posed no conceivable threat to the IRA or their cause. He had pursued a remarkable career in the Royal Navy; had avenged the execration unjustly heaped on his German-born father during World War I by assuming, decades later, his mantle of First Sea Lord; had contracted a brilliant, if sometimes tumultuous marriage; and had overseen the problematical and dangerous transition of India from imperial dominion to independent, though divided, nation. After such an active and successful life, it might have been argued that the fading and debilitating years of extreme old age would not have been for him. Yet the manner of his death horrified the world, and the sheer disbelief it prompted among those least conscious of or touched by his many achievements testified to the mute realisation that in this so-called civilised century, unspeakable dangers lurked even for the least influential of public figures, and that being royal was certainly no guarantee of exemption from peril.

Lord Mountbatten was as exact a contemporary as you could wish to find of that other long-established royal figure, Queen Elizabeth the Queen Mother – indeed they were born within six weeks of each other in the dying months of Queen Victoria's long reign. It seemed a cruel stroke of fate that deprived Mountbatten of being associated in 1980 with the warm and appreciative celebration of the Queen Mother's eightieth birthday. Though it involved a glowing service of thanksgiving in St Paul's Cathedral, elegant processions of landaus and princes on horseback, a balcony appearance, and official photographs before and on the chosen day, it was no formal State occasion, but rather a pleasant mid-summer jubilee for a much-loved grannie figure. Since her widowhood almost thirty years before, the Queen Mother had gone about her private and public business with that sense of purpose which was the foundation of her strong character, but at the same time in the knowledge that, because the reins of constitutional power lay with her daughter, many of her own coming and goings must remain comparatively unsung, if not exactly unheralded. For all that she revels in a little bit of fuss – and she certainly got it on that July day in 1980 – the Queen Mother has since 1952 been resigned to taking second place, even if she may occasionally reflect that fate cheated her of the full reward of those long years of dedication and anxiety when the Crown and the country were successively in a less secure condition.

With all the plaudits she received as she entered her octagenarian years, she might well have felt justified in calling a halt to her 57 years of public service. Indeed, for some time beforehand the number of her engagements had been dwindling. Time has, however, proved anyone wrong who thought retirement near. The ghost of Queen Mary, who did not consider one's duty fully accomplished with the coming of any birthday, no matter how advanced, seems still to haunt the royal palaces and keep their occupants up to the mark. So her successor as Queen Consort and dowager has now passed the half-way mark to her nineties, and is still going strong. Tolerant of modern trends and fashions yet resolutely loyal to her own, selective of acquaintance and fast of friendship, an inspiration in her time to all four of her grandchildren, bothered only occasionally by illness, notoriously unpunctual, a warm and sincere speaker, a vintage charmer with time and patience to spare, she has probably never enjoyed life so much as she does now. And on June 3rd, 1986, she became the longest lived Queen Consort in British history.

But not quite the oldest member of the Royal Family – yet. That distinction belonged to Princess Alice, Countess of Athlone who died at the beginning of 1981, within seven weeks of her 98th birthday. The daughter of the haemophiliac Prince Leopold, youngest son of Queen Victoria, Princess Alice gave her only television interview in 1975, at the age of 93, and painted a fascinating picture of her early life at Court – when the ageing Queen used to dispense gold sovereigns from a coral and gold bag for every tooth her grandchildren could claim to have lost; when the family visited Germany and were subjected to the Kaiser's pompous, stiff hospitality; when Alice's brother was sick in the royal carriage during Queen Victoria's Diamond Jubilee procession; and when the Queen's funeral horses refused to pull her hearse and had to be replaced with a contingent of naval cadets. In those days, she said, every member of the family was expected to behave with the utmost decorum and correctness. 'People are watching,' she was told. 'You're doing this for the Queen.'

In essence, things have changed little in the nine decades that have followed. People are still watching, though with less insistence on those impeccable, stiff-upper-lip niceties that nowadays make Victorian standards of behaviour appear faintly ridiculous. And the Royal Family are still doing this, that and the other thing, very much for the Queen.

On the day before what would have been Princess Alice's 98th birthday, Prince Charles announced his engagement to Lady Diana Spencer. The wedding that took place the following July may not have been quite the equal of Queen Victoria's Diamond Jubilee service, but for the 750 million people watching the ceremony and celebrations world-wide, it may not have fallen far short. The story of the Royal Family continues with this young couple and their two delightful children shaping up to the prospect of Prince Charles' kingship and all that it entails for them personally and for those many royal relatives who will be expected to maintain their supporting roles for the future Charles III as they are doing for Elizabeth II.

The last five years of that story unfolds in the following pages, in the blaze of colour which sets royal events and personalities apart from the routine daily round which the rest of us tolerate with or without cheerfulness. If that one truth should jar, remember that, for all their privileges – from the untaxed wealth to the opportunity to travel the world almost at the touch of a button – the Queen and her family have responsibilities which are not only official but also uncomfortably personal. If you have ever said you wouldn't have their job for all the tea in China, you may have been reflecting that there may be more than a few disadvantages in a lifestyle which prevents you from remaining anonymous in a crowd, or being truly alone within your own four security-surrounded walls, or doing what you like, when you like, how you like. Hopping on a bus, spending real money, and not knowing quite what's round the corner may be considered positive freedoms when we realise that, unlike them, we can do all these things without having to watch for sneak photographers, confer with ubiquitous equerries and advisors, consult time-schedules, map out our lives in detail for at least two years in advance, maintain a permanent toothpaste smile and keep the conversation going at all costs. Rather them than me? It's a sobering thought.

Where to begin and end any account of a year in the life of the British Royal Family? It is tempting to plump for the calendar year as the safest and most easily recognisable period, but the long and unashamedly leisurely royal vacation at Balmoral provides cogent evidence that the Queen at least sees her public year as starting in October and finishing the following July. There is a case for treating the Queen's official birthday, traditionally celebrated on the second Saturday in June, as the event which divides one year from the next: this was indeed the basis on which the one and only comprehensive and authorised film about a typical royal year – *Royal Family*, shown in the run-up to the Investiture of Prince Charles as Prince of Wales in July 1969 – was produced.

A fixed event like Trooping the

organisers for whom this is truly a once-a-year occasion; the stall holders whose harvest of customers must be attracted to what they have to sell; the fairground which makes a mint of money out of the fact that the Derby has long since become a family occasion on which children have to be catered for as fully as their parents. The nervous tension belongs, and is the prerogative of, the small army of owners, trainers, stable-lads, grooms and, by no means least of all, the jockeys. For all of them, an enterprise which began as much as four years before, when the sires and dams of today's runners were mated almost specifically with this occasion in mind, comes to fruition. The result of the race determines not only the destination of over £200,000 worth of prize money, but also the stud value of every horse

Colour is probably the best candidate of the three, punctuating the year as it does with the unchanging and normally triumphant celebration of a royal tribute by a resplendent militia in full ceremonial dress. Equally unchanging is the annual Derby meeting. Epsom in early June of 1981 provided a major

focal point, even for just one afternoon, for so many people – royalty and commoners, British and foreign, sporting and spectating, serious-minded and fun-seeking – and we have chosen that event to begin our chronicle of five years of colourful happenings, both local, national and international, over which the Queen, as Head of

State, and her family in its supporting role have presided. The Derby, held every year on Epsom Downs, has never lost its grip on the public imagination. Off the course and outside the specialised and highly commercial confines of the world of thoroughbred breeding, the event attracts the speculation of millions of ordinary men and women, who on this occasion as on no other sink many more millions of pounds into what is sometimes, if a little unkindly, called the bookmakers' benevolent fund.

On and around the course, the day itself is one of feverish activity and tensed nerves. The feverish activity is that of the

taking part. A victory at this most especial of Britain's five Classic races puts the winner into such demand as a stallion, that £10 million is these days a cheap price to pay for him. The Queen, seeking the first Derby win for a member of her family in over three quarters of a century, declared her own entry, which she does as often as not. His name was Church Parade and the Queen's reservations about his chances of success seemed to be evidenced by the fleeting, uncertain looks on her normally relaxed features as the proceedings got under way on 3rd June. Appearances had to be kept up, however, and she arrived, accompanied by the

...een Mother (opposite page, ...), smiling brightly as the ...torcade crept silently up the ...urse.

...shion-wise, 1981 seemed to be ...e year in which deep, bright ...lours took the place of paler ...ades and subtle pastels, as the ...een was obviously aware. Red ...s clearly the royal favourite, ...th Princess Alexandra wearing ...most exactly the same shade as ...e Queen, in an outfit broken ...ly by a lacy frill which Lady ...ana Spencer had already made ...pular. The Duchess of ...oucester (next to Princess ...exandra in the picture, ...pposite page, right) wore a ...milar deep red to set off her ...nk suit. The Queen's warm, ...ic cherry-red outfit was one of

weeks brought the five-months-long preparations for the century's most spectacular wedding to its brilliant and triumphal climax. The Queen's tour of Australasia and Sri Lanka found parallels in her son and daughter-in-law's successful visit to their Principality in October, and the news a week later that the new Princess of Wales was expecting her first baby brought an unexpected bonus to this year of celebration, and gave everyone something to look forward to in 1982.
Not that 1982 was short on incident. The quite sudden eruption of the crisis in the Falkland Islands provided the political and patriotic talking point of the year, and the Royal

...er personal favourites: she had ...ready worn it at Royal Ascot ...e previous year, and for her ...ate Visit to Switzerland: it ...ould be seen again in New ...ealand in October and at ...hichester as late as July 1982. ...y contrast, the Queen Mother ...ted for a quiet off-white coat ...d hat (above) while Princess ...ichael kept to the bright side

with a crisp, pure-white, close-fitting coat and small saucer-shaped hat (above, far left). These royal fashions could be seen during those few minutes when the Queen and her family came down from the Royal Box to inspect the runners from the side of the course shortly before the Derby itself. The Queen's expression gave nothing away, and she was in events right not to have betrayed too much optimism. Church Parade came fifth – a creditable showing, but one which leaves the Queen with horse-racing ambitions to fulfil.
The 1981 Derby heralded a year of almost unprecedented activity for the Royal Family. Just over a week later came the drama of the now notorious incident during the Trooping the Colour ceremonial, and the following

Family were not isolated from its consequences. From the departure of Prince Andrew in the *Invincible* at the beginning of April to the services of commemoration and charity galas in aid of the dependants of the fallen, the entire Family was in one way or another involved from start to finish.
To crown the success of the campaign, the birth of Prince William justified the national celebration. His christening on 4th August, the Queen Mother's 82nd birthday, provided an apt reminder of the continuity of monarchy, reinforced to date by Prince Harry's birth, the coming of age of several of his cousins, the Queen's 60th and the Queen Mother's 85th birthdays, and a profusion of colourful royal events at home and abroad.

Guards celebrated her official birthday with the annual ceremony of Trooping the Colour.

The day began pleasantly enough, with large crowds – certainly larger than usual even on this occasion – lining the Mall and filling the stands on Horse Guards Parade, ready and waiting to enjoy the almost unchanging ritual at the height of a benign summer's weather. The Queen, mounted side-saddle on her mare Burmese, had stood at the main gates of Buckingham Palace to watch her Guards pass by on their way to Horse Guards, and eventually she took her place in the colourful procession down the

The happy mood of anticipation of the climax of 1981's royal events was startlingly marred by the dramatic events, almost unprecedented this century, which took place on Saturday 13th June – the day on which the Queen's Household Brigades of

Mall, cheered on by thousands of people exuberant with the splendour of the occasion. Just before the procession reached Admiralty Arch, at the Trafalgar Square end of the Mall, it turned right into a short approach road which links the

Mall to Horse Guards Parade. It was at this junction that, as the Queen herself passed, six pistol shots rang out loud and clear from the midst of the crowd. Burmese made an uncontrollable skittish movement which in its suddenness jerked the Queen momentarily off balance, but even riding side-saddle she reacted quickly enough to bring the mare under almost immediate control.

While a mêlée of spectators jostled and fought with the assailant, two or three streetliners – members of the Guards' regiments detailed to line the processional route for the occasion – joined in the fray and dozens of police teemed across the roadway to make their arrest. The procession was thrown into only temporary disorder and continued to make its way to its destination.

Towards its head the Queen, looking quite alarmingly drained

of colour, was giving her mount reassuring pats on the neck, while Prince Charles, who had been riding immediately behind her, trotted up to reassure her that the assailant had been seized.

In fact the man was lucky to be alive at all, such was the outrage felt by nearby spectators and the particular fury of one Guardsman who confessed afterwards to having been so angry that he very nearly used his bayonet on him. As it soon became clear the assault did not amount to an assassination attempt: the pistol fired at or towards the Queen carried only blank rounds, and its owner 17-year-old Marcus Serjeant had, it seemed, intended no harm to the Queen. It transpired, however, during the ensuing criminal trial, in which Serjeant was indicted for firing a gun with intent to alarm the Queen, that he had made several efforts to

obtain live ammunition, had boasted several times to his friends and neighbours that he would do something to make himself famous, and had even written to the Queen to warn her not to leave Buckingham Palace on 13th June as "there is an assassin set up to kill you." He was found guilty and sent to jail for five years.

It was ironic that on this of all occasions the Queen should have been so utterly vulnerable whilst in the presence of such a huge contingent of her personal bodyguard. It was also gratifying that she was so wholly in command of the situation that the procession and the entire ceremony continued without

giving anyone who had not witnessed or heard of the incident the slightest cause for suspicion or unease. For those people, some 8,000 of them, lining the parade ground the military spectacle lived up to expectations throughout, and went on as smoothly as the previous week's rehearsal when Prince Charles took the Salute (left, below left and opposite page top centre). It had the bonus, of course, of being preceded by the usual royal ceremonial arrivals: the Queen Mother and Princess Margaret in one landau and Prince Andrew and Lady Diana Spencer in the other. And the crowds at Buckingham Palace

end knew nothing as they cheered the Queen back to the Palace, and again when she came out onto the balcony (opposite page, centre) for the traditional R.A.F. fly-past. The Queen showed no tension either, as she was joined by some of the younger members of her family – Lord Nicholas Windsor, son of the Duke of Kent, and Lady Davina Windsor and her brother the Earl of Ulster, the children of the Duke of Gloucester.

The Most Noble Order of the Garter is the oldest Order of Chivalry in the Kingdom. It was founded in 1348 by King Edward III as a fusion of the two ideals upon which he of all monarchs genuinely strove to establish a stable régime – military strength and religious fervour. Membership of the Order was then confined to the twenty-five most outstanding military leaders, who remained in close fellowship with their Sovereign and with each other for the rest of their days. But the three-day gathering each year – originally around St George's Day on 23rd April, brought them together personally for religious worship "to the honour of Almighty God, the glorious Virgin Saint Mary and St George the Martyr."

Like most ceremonies of ancient origin, the Garter has been the subject of neglect, change and rejuvenation throughout the six centuries of its existence. In

Tudor and Jacobean times the Festival was allowed to lapse occasionally and St George's Day was not always chosen as the precise time of celebration. Services for the installation of new Knights were hardly ever held in the entire course of the

eteenth century. King George
 deep-seated sense of
dition prompted him to
ntroduce many of its facets,
 it was his son and successor
ng George VI who, in
ebration of the six-hundredth
niversary of the Order's
uguration, arranged for an
embly of Knights to meet,
cess to and attend a Service
St George's Chapel, Windsor
stle on 23rd April 1948.
e ceremony we know today
tes from that time, and 1981's

proceedings, held on 15th June,
possessed the added attraction
of the attendance of Lady Diana
Spencer (below, far left and
opposite page, top right) who
experienced the solemnity and
spectacle of the service for the
first time. She was accompanied
by Lady Susan Hussey (pictured
opposite page, bottom, in gold
hat), the Queen's senior lady in
waiting, who was responsible for
preparing Lady Diana for her
future role.

There are years when it is forgiveable to imagine that Royal Ascot can do quite well without its royalty. It is very often a social beano that has little or nothing to do with horses, and the preoccupation with the size of hats or the length of skirts, the obsession with socialising for its own sake against a mere background of high quality flat racing is not relieved by Fleet Street's continuing search for the catchy news item or the pictorial scoop which satisfies readers' curiosity and panders to exhibitionism. When these elements are not only present but also prominent, the royal presence seems like a respectable covering over a not very professionally-baked cake. But there have been times when the royal flavour has been strong and authoritative. Black Ascot in

1936 was a particularly striking occasion, when anyone who was anyone signified their mourning for the death of King George V not by foregoing Royal Ascot, but by wearing black on all four days of the meeting. There was genuine excitement at Ascot in 1953, not just because it was held in the same month as the Coronation but also because, in the wake of the superb performance put on by the Queen's horse Aureole in the Derby just a fortnight before, the feeling was that this year must surely be the Queen's year on the racecourse.
1981 was another such year because of the appearance of the Royal Family's potential new recruit, Lady Diana Spencer, now within six weeks of her magnificent and historic wedding. Like the Queen and

demure blush, the lowering of the eyes, following rather than leading where behaviour counted most. Fashion-wise she strove not to outshine. On the first day of Royal Ascot, 16th June, she wore a soft mauve an

the Queen Mother, Lady Diana attended the meeting on all four days and there was never any doubting that she was the cynosure of all eyes. Whether this was through envy, curiosity, protectiveness or admiration mattered not. She had arrived and to prove it she was there. But she maintained the modest, restrained attitude – the famous

gold striped outfit with a plain, semi-platter hat trimmed with ostrich feather (above) – one of her favourite types of adornmen in 1981, under the Belleville Sassoon influence. On the second day (top left) she was in an equally delicate peach top and skirt, and sporting a generous fold of material round the neck as a variation of the fril

while Prince Charles was away. He had to miss the middle two days of the meeting in order to pay a visit to the United States to attend a charity gala. But Lady Diana's training for her future role was nothing if not thorough, and when Prince Charles was not available Princess Alexandra (below left) or a personal detective (opposite page far left) or the Queen Mother (overleaf) was. Few public events offered more opportunity to accustom oneself to the sight of huge, admiring, scrutinising crowds, and if Lady Diana harboured any doubts about her ability to cope in front of so many thousands they were dispelled during this one week of Royal Ascot. She was the universal favourite. Prince Charles had picked well.

or ruff which she had already made her hallmark. Day three saw her in a sharp, striking ensemble – bright red lightweight clothes, setting off an expansive candy-striped blouse with a huge bow finishing off another broad, flat ruff (opposite page far left). And on the last day she wore a more subdued dress in blue and white squares with a light, saucer-shaped hat tied down in the Edwardian style with net brought under the chin (above and right). No extremes of fashion here, but a million tall girls up and down the country thanked her for making the flat shoe almost a status symbol. It may have raised some eyebrows that Lady Diana continued to attend Royal Ascot

It was only natural that Lady Diana should appear to have eclipsed the Royal Family, who themselves turned out in force for Royal Ascot. She had, after all, enjoyed (in the most neutral sense of the word) enormous choice typical of someone basically unsure of herself in her new surroundings. They also mistook her amusing interludes with children and fits of giggling on royal walkabouts as signs that she could not cope with the

publicity since the very earliest days of her courtship almost a year previously; and the great publicity machine, to some extent and understandably encouraged by the Palace in preparation for the Wedding of the Century, had not yet produced all it was capable of in terms of the projection of this new celebrity onto the national screen.

Because of her background and her lifestyle she was portrayed as one in need of protection, vulnerable and fragile, about to be thrown in at the deep end. Those who did not admire her daringly low-cut black taffeta evening gown on her first official appearance considered the

formality of her future life, and they found her choice of clothe precociously mature.

By May, when visits like the on to Broadlands made it clear tha she had no intention of changin her ways and that, moreover, th public liked what they saw, the general attitude changed, and the reams of advice which commentators in the Press had been dispensing liberally and often began to peter out. She was at last becoming unquestioningly accepted and very, ver popular. No wonder all eyes were upon her as Society's mos colourful race-meeting got underway.

Nevertheless her future in-laws were also there and gave Ascot

unforgettable and almost
changeable degree of status. If
val Ascot is the by-word for
ssive hats, however, it can be
ed authoritatively that none
his reputation can be traced
he Royal Family. As these
tures show, its members
nd stylishly, as the occasion
nands, but in the same or
ilar outfits to those worn to
official function. The
een's blue dress and
tching hat with its white
nelia (top right) would thus
seen twice on her
thcoming Australasian tour;
ncess Margaret's ensemble,
ped with a white-plumed
an (above) would be worn,
st appropriately, at the

celebrations to mark the King of
Swaziland's sixty years' reign in
September, and the Queen
Mother wore the same sunny
yellow outfit (right) at a service
for the Friends of St Paul's
Cathedral in July.
But then, the Royal Family
comes to Ascot to enjoy the
racing much more than to
indulge in fashionable
escapades. It is a dyed-in-the-
wool family tradition which even
Prince Philip, who (opposite
page centre left) rarely looks
entirely at ease there, is content
to acknowledge by his
occasional presence.

occasion will be remembered, thanks to the meticulous arrangements by Lord Maclean, for going exactly according to plan, for the superb selection of music chosen by the royal couple and for the faultless timing of every element in the complex timetable of procedures. Security was necessarily strong but pleasantly unobtrusive; arrests took place in single figures only, and for deeds no more anarchic than street-trading or pickpocketing. The seventy-minute-long service, held, unlike any comparable royal wedding since 1501, in St Paul's Cathedral, crystallised everything

The wedding of the Prince and Princess of Wales on 29th July 1981 outshone all previous royal events, with the possible exception of the Queen's Coronation, in terms of colour, spectacle, the acknowledgement of tradition and the depth and sincerity of popular acclaim. In a year which had seen its fair share of domestic troubles the

memorable: the fluffed lines from bride and groom, the Speaker's melodramatic reading of the Lesson, the Archbishop's short address, as cleverly designed as his new ice-blue cape and mitre, the restless fidgeting of the younger bridesmaids, the gradual relaxation in the Queen's demeanour, the occasional tear on the Queen Mother's cheek. Like all wedding days it was very much the bride's hour, and her superb puffed dress of ivory silk encrusted with a thousand sequins and mother of pearl embedded in fussy lace panels and frills, reinforced her claim to popular attention. As Lady Diana she was cheered to the echo on leaving Clarence House in the Glass Coach, and as Princess of Wales the return journey was positively deafening. The symbol and one lasting memory of the day was the now

celebrated balcony kiss – a rare moment of royal spontaneity on a formal occasion. The official photographs were much more studied, for the most part, though Lord Lichfield captured a couple of moments of sheer fun. And balloons on the going-away carriage extended the sense of fun to the end.

The honeymoon began at Broadlands. No pictures exist save those taken privately on the last morning of the stay; some of them are on display at the mansion itself. No concession was made to the demands of publicity after the most public of courtships and the most universally witnessed of weddings. Three days of peace and serenity on English soil were all the Prince and Princess asked and, in the haven which great-uncle Mountbatten had made his own, and where his nephew the Duke of Edinburgh had taken his bride in 1947, the royal couple got it. Around them was

indeed a large part – was for the couple personally but there could be no doubt that the islanders were taking every opportunity to reaffirm their British sympathies in the face of Spanish attempts to take control of Gibraltar and the refusal of King Juan Carlos to attend the Royal Wedding in protest against this very day's proceedings. The 40-minute drive to the quayside in a borrowed Triumph Stag was an emotional experience for everyone (bottom left) and the farewells were sincere and quite moving (below, and bottom pictures). Alone at last they spent twelve days

a strong security presence: within they were with discreet friends and had the use of a 6,000-acre estate in the heart of Hampshire.
On 1st August they travelled to Eastleigh Airport to fly to Gibraltar for the beginning of the foreign leg of the honeymoon. Prince Charles piloted an Andover of the Queen's Flight, leaving his wife as a passenger in the same way that he had, it was rumoured, left her at Broadlands one morning while he went fishing for trout in the Test.
The flight lasted four hours and the royal arrival was wildly feted in a town vibrant with red white and blue. Part of the welcome –

soaking up the sun and visiting one Mediterranean island after another from the Royal Yacht *Britannia* (opposite page top). They swam and windsurfed, toured and explored until on 12th August they reached Egypt as guests of the ill-fated President Sadat. Seven weeks after they took their leave, he was dead, and Prince Charles was again in Cairo to pay his last respects.

But all were unsuspecting at Balmoral when on 19th August the Prince and Princess met the Press at the Brig O'Dee (this page). And even the Princess agreed that it was "one of the best places in the world."

One of the most tactful and well-received royal decisions of 1981 was that the Prince and Princess of Wales would begin their public life's work together with a three-day visit to Wales itself. After a prolonged holiday at Balmoral, during which the only public engagement they undertook was the traditional royal attendance at the Braemar Gathering early in September, it seemed not only desirable but also a natural consequence of

Castle (left and below far left) where Prince Charles was ceremonially invested as Prince of Wales in July 1969. Here they were met formally – and informally (below and below left) by Lord Snowdon as Constable of the Castle. After spending an hour there, they were off to Bangor and Plas

their position and title that they should choose the Principality as the venue of their first public engagements.

Their schedule was one of the sort normally associated with State visits; eleven or twelve hours each day, excluding travelling time to the first engagement and from the last. Lunch never exceeded an hour. With eighteen towns to visit it was very much a whistle-stop tour, reminiscent of Gladstone's election campaigns.

On 27th October the Prince and Princess paid visits to Deeside Leisure Centre (above) and Shotton, Rhyl and Caernarfon

wydd, rounding off a day
ch surprised even the Press
its popular enthusiasm.
d of North Wales' reception
pted the people of the
h-west of the Principality to
out in vast numbers the
wing day. They watched the
l couple visit St David's
edral (opposite page,
bottom left) for a service which
revealed that the Princess had
not yet learned very much
Welsh, and they stood in
pouring rain to greet them at
Haverfordwest, Carmarthen and
Llandeilo. A superb gala concert
at Swansea, after which the
Princess was surrounded by
youngsters offering gifts (bottom

left and centre), completed a
hectic second day.

The final day, 29th October,
brought the tour to the South
where the public response was
at its wildest. The day began
with the opening of the Young
Farmers' Club at the Royal
Welsh Showground at
Llanelwedd (far left) and there
were subsequent walkabouts in
Pontypridd (left) and Brecon
(below and bottom). During a

visit to Llwynypia Hospital the
Prince and Princess inspected
the maternity wing and Prince
Charles spoke of the benefits of
fathers seeing their children
born. His words hit the next
day's papers, though no-one
suspected the news of the
Princess' own pregnancy, which
was announced to a delighted
nation the following week.

Since reaching 80 in December 1981, Princess Alice has often resolved to reduce her tally of engagements. But that's easier said than done: "The trouble is that when you have been associated with organisations for many years and someone pleads with you to do something you did for them last year, or they say it's all going to be a terrible flop if you don't go, what can you do?" Her staff see it differently, marvelling as she finds excuses to do things which a less resolute octogenarian would happily dodge.

She is probably as unconvinced of her age as anyone meeting her would be. A lively mind, a deceptive sense of humour and a phenomenal memory belie her 85 years every bit as much as her impeccable deportment and the straight back which, though her figure is much more petite, recall her mother-in-law Queen Mary.

Her memory goes back to the age of two or three, but, she warned "the story is too silly to relate." She remembers her sheer terror when, while being bathed one evening, the nursery door burst open. In tumbled two elder brothers, full of mischief, and a great boot landed "with a terrible splash" into the bathtub! A more embarrassing incident

befell when she and a younger sister were to present a single bouquet of flowers – "a fatal thing to arrange" – to Princess Louise, Duchess of Argyll when she opened the Hydropathic Institution at Melrose. At the last moment her sister suddenly shouted "I don't like *her*," snatched the bouquet away and presented it to someone else. Lady Alice Montagu-Douglas-Scott's childhood was typical of the Edwardian aristocracy: governesses, nannies and the constant shifting between her father's three residences. Her mother was reserved and, it seems, rather a distant figure: her father, Duke of Buccleuch, an MP and Lord Lieutenant, was busy, little seen by his children, and immensely authoritarian. Even in her twenties he refused her an allowance for her to go to East Africa, so she held an exhibition of her paintings and used the proceeds for the trip. They were exciting days; she took photographs of wildlife which won prizes when she got back home.

Life changed considerably after she married the Duke of Gloucester, King George V's third son, in 1935. They were quietly devoted to each other and she was warmly welcomed into the family. The King, then very sick man, was "very kind to me," and Queen Mary used to invite her over to Marlborough House of an evening when the

Duke was away. King George VI kindly wrote to her in 1942, when the Duke was abroad, "Do let me know when you want to come and stay at Windsor."

Her public life took her to most parts of the world, but Barnwell, her country home in Northamptonshire, is her haven. "Our weekends are very precious," she says, and these pictures of her with her three grandchildren (opposite page) say it all. She still shines on duty, as (opposite page top right) at Crosby Hall, a student residence in Chelsea, on 17th March, and was thrilled at

having her 80th birthday honoured by the presentation of a new rose, Blesma Soul, to her at Kensington Palace on 6th January (this page).

Her birthday fell on Christmas Day, when the entire Royal Family was at Windsor. Did she have a party? She checked a hollow laugh: "There's *always* a party. Princess Alexandra and I shared the cake!"

One of the earliest royal engagements of 1982 was the visit by Prince and Princess Michael of Kent to St Paul's Cathedral to attend the Inaugural Celebration of the English Tourist Board's "Maritime England" Promotion. The promotion consists of over two thousand events which have and will continue to take place throughout England in 1982, from art exhibitions to sand castle competitions, regattas to concerts – all on a maritime theme.

The Inaugural Celebration was held on 14th January with a concert of music descriptive of, or connected with, the sea. Nine items made up the whole, with Mendelssohn's overture "Calm Sea and Prosperous Voyage," and the opening sequence from

Vaughan-Williams' "Sea Symphony" alternating with sea songs and naval miscellanies. It seemed that no expense was spared to give the event its initial lift: the Royal Philharmonic Orchestra was joined by the Band of the Royal Marines; the Bach Choir, with the Duchess of Kent as one of its members, performed as well, as did the Fanfare Trumpeters and Corps of Drums, who had previously performed at the Prince of Wales' Wedding in July. The Master of Ceremonies for the evening was BBC TV's newsreader and music lover Richard Baker.

"The Michaels," as Prince and Princess Michael are informally known, gave the concert that air of royal informality which creates enjoyment out of any

imposing occasion. The Czech born Princess, formerly Baroness von Reibnitz, sported one of her favourite lines in headgear, a petite, bowler-style veiled hat, while her husband was able to show off a beard of more luxuriant growth than ever before. It was the second time he had grown a beard since his marriage; this most recent attempt began in August and first came to public notice when he and Princess Michael went to Belize in September, on behalf of the Queen, to preside over the gaining of independence from Britain. Rarely is an opportunity missed to comment on how like he is to his grandfather King George V, but in an age when few royal princes grow beards, everything is relative. Perhaps it depends

on what light you catch him

nce Michael has now quit
ive service in the Army – he
ired from the Royal Hussars
h the rank of Major in March
1. He has, however, obtained
mission from the Queen to
ntinue to wear uniform, and
l so for the Royal Wedding
following July. He now has
re time to spend attending
icial functions: indeed during
1 he and his wife clocked up
fewer than 120. These were
stly in London as their
penses have to be met from
ir own private funds. Since
ince Michael, seven years
junior of his brother the
ke of Kent, is only the
inger son of the Kent
nily, he does not undertake
icial duties and has not

within the Church of England
and their places in the line of
succession are assured. It is
however unlikely that they will
be called upon to perform
official duties, since the Kent
family is already well represented
by the Duke of Kent and his two
sons. In addition of course, as
the Queen's own children
produce families who will
ultimately take up the more
important royal duties, the
pressure will be lifted from both
the Gloucesters and the Kents
who, representing King George
V's younger sons, have been
sharing the royal round with the

been entitled to receive any Civil
List payments – nor do his and
his wife's attendances at official
functions warrant a mention in
the Court Circular.
Prince and Princess Michael's
two children, Lord Frederick
Windsor, born in April 1979, and
Lady Gabriella, born in April
1981, are both being brought up

Queen and her more immediate
family. By then both Lord
Frederick and Lady Gabriella,
now 20th and 21st respectively
in the line of succession, will
have been pushed so far down as
to make it only academically
possible for them to succeed to
the Throne.

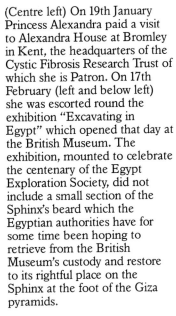

(Centre left) On 19th January Princess Alexandra paid a visit to Alexandra House at Bromley in Kent, the headquarters of the Cystic Fibrosis Research Trust of which she is Patron. On 17th February (left and below left) she was escorted round the exhibition "Excavating in Egypt" which opened that day at the British Museum. The exhibition, mounted to celebrate the centenary of the Egypt Exploration Society, did not include a small section of the Sphinx's beard which the Egyptian authorities have for some time been hoping to retrieve from the British Museum's custody and restore to its rightful place on the Sphinx at the foot of the Giza pyramids.

(Opposite page) Princess Alexandra in animated mood when she attended a fashion show at the Japanese Embassy residence in London on 25th January. The show, presented by designer Hanai Mori, was staged in aid of the Mental Health Foundation of which the Princess is Patron. She and her husband, the Hon Angus Ogilvy, were treated to a long succession of vivid and elegant designs, drawn from many different national cultures and betraying influences of fashions past and present (right).

The Princess' 1982 engagements began somewhat earlier than those of most members of the Royal Family, and January was a comparatively busy month.

Penlee is one of those names which, unknown to 99% of Britain's population for generations, suddenly becomes a household word for decades. It is to the history of the sea what Lewisham and Harrow are to the railways, Aberfan to the coal industry, Flixborough to the chemical industry. On 19th December 1981, in the grip of one of the iciest autumns for years, a coaster, the *Union Star,* listing helplessly in mountainous seas, tried in vain to reach shelter on the South Cornish coast. In an attempt to save the eight people on board, the Penlee lifeboat *Solomon Browne* set out in impossible weather and amid a confusion of signals from the distressed ship. Her mission was doomed: the lifeboat was pushed remorselessly towards the rocks where in

men to their deaths. The church, which overlooks the stricken village, had three of the dead crew buried in its churchyard, and the RNLI flag fluttered noisily at half mast as the Duke and Duchess arrived to be greeted by a guard of honour made up of 25 life-boatmen, some of them related to the victims of the disaster. Inside were five hundred local people, crammed in as nothing before witnessed there. A further 200 people huddled together in a marquee to which the service was relayed. RNLI branches throughout Britain had requested places for represen-tatives, but had to be told that the service was strictly limited to local interest and that room for wider public condolence would be available at a memorial service to be held at Truro

heaving seas she was smashed to pieces. Eight of her volunteer crew died, and in that one terrible venture five women were widowed and a dozen children rendered fatherless.

In the wake of the immediate tragedy, help came from all parts of the country. Even before an enquiry could get under way a voluntary fund was set up and thousands of pounds poured in to help the bereaved families and set the tiny village community back on its feet again. On 22nd January, the 81st anniversary of one death – that of Queen Victoria – which unleashed national grief of a different kind, the Duke of Kent, as President of the Royal National Lifeboat Institution, and the Duchess of Kent, attended a Family Service of Remembrance and Thanks-giving in the Parish Church in Mousehole.

It was a sharp, windswept day, but the skies were blue and little indication existed of the monstrous conditions which only a month before had sent

Cathedral the following month. The service lasted barely three quarters of an hour, and was very simple. The Duke of Kent read the lesson and a local television personality, Mr Clive Gunnell, gave an address praising selflessness and preferring the regenerative spirit to the cold stone memorial. When it was all over the Duke and Duchess, accompanied by

the Vicar, the Reverend Hugh Cadman, went to the vicarage to meet the bereaved families privately. The Duchess, clutching a wrapped bunch of flowers presented to her there, assured them that her sympathy was with them all. "I hope this is a day you will never forget, but also a day that will never come again," she said. To Mrs Mary Greenhalgh, whose husband's

th had left her as licensee of
Ship Inn, the Duchess made
promise that when she was
in Cornwall on holiday she
uld come to her pub and
e a drink. Both the Duke
the Duchess gave full rein to
only sentiment they could
sibly contribute. "They were
y sympathetic and expressed
hope that we would be able
ick up the threads of our
s," said one woman. The
ke was poignantly impressed.
was a deeply moving
vice," he said. "It was
gnificent to meet the families.
y showed so much courage

and were such a great
inspiration."
Since that solemn royal day
the courage has continued.
Funds poured in from all
parts of the country and beyond
its shores. A new contingent of
men from Penlee and
Mousehole have offered
themselves as replacements for
their lost neighbours in the
unending and invaluable service
of the RNLI. Slowly, and not
without the distress which
fundamental readjustment in the
full glare of publicity invariably
brings, life has begun to assume
something approaching normality.
But the personal tragedy lives
on, with a severity which blights
each succeeding birthday,
wedding anniversary and
Christmas celebration with its
persistent reminder that a loved
one is irretrievably absent.
Only after other national and
international calamities had

overwhelmed the horror of
Penlee could its widows and
orphans grieve privately at
last. But they were touched
by the memory of that royal
involvement in that very hour
when the need for consolation
and moral support was greatest.
For one afternoon this short but
heartfelt royal visit brought the
nation's attention to the plight of
one of its smallest villages, bereft
of a proportion of its manhood
which in a major city would have
been regarded as a national
disaster. Here and now the
disaster existed only within the
heart of a tiny community where
no-one remained unaffected by
the reality of what lifeboatmen
the world over regard as an
occupational hazard.

On 2nd February Queen Elizabeth the Queen Mother undertook her second public engagement of 1982 when she visited Canada House to open its new Cultural Centre. After her arrival she was taken up to the High Commissioner's Office for a short private meeting. A quarter of an hour later she came down the stairs (below) escorted by the High Commissioner Mrs Jean Casselman Wadds (below right) and led by a piper – Lieutenant Mike Ward of the Royal Canadian Dragoons. Once into the auditorium at the foot of the stairs, she declared the Cultural Centre open and received a vote of thanks from the Canadian Minister of Culture and Public Affairs, Mr John Graham.

The ceremony was short but it kept alive the Queen Mother's links with Canada which were forged almost forty-three years before. In 1939, less than three years after their accession, she accompanied King George VI on an exhausting and comprehensive 6-week State Visit there, which took them from coast to coast, and eclipsed even the brilliant State Visit to France the previous year. It was nearly written off when their ship *Empress of Australia* almost hit an iceberg at about the spot where *HMS Titanic* foundered in 1912, and almost on the anniversary of the tragedy. But the royal arrival at Quebec on 17th May 1939 made King George VI the first reigning British sovereign to tread on the soil of what was then fondly known as British North America. The tour was a resounding success. Travel was mostly by

the "silver and blue train" as it was familiarly known – a 300-ton blue and aluminium CPR locomotive pulling twelve streamlined coaches over a total of more than 9,000 miles in the course of the six-week tour from Quebec to Vancouver and back to Halifax. At every station – and with a full programme which left very little time for relaxation there were many stations – there was a crowd to greet the King and Queen. Like most tours this one had its formal and informal moments. For the Queen, the laying of the foundation stone for the new Supreme Court building in Ottawa was perhaps the most memorable. She mused on the fact that she, and not the King, had been asked to lay the stone,

but concluded that the choice was appropriate as "woman's position in modern society ha depended upon the growth of law." Amongst the more infor interludes was the private visi see the famous Dionne quins who had been born in Canada six years earlier. The Queen herself was credited with miraculous powers when, despite persistent rain during drive through Winnipeg, she instructed that the car's roof should be let down so that people could see her. Almost immediately the rain stopped! But she seemed to have enou personal magic of her own. As one commentator said, "As fo the Queen she appeared and day was won. So simple in her bearing and yet so refined, so spontaneous in every move ar yet so harmonious; so radiant with feminine charm and so expressive of emotion, she als found the true words for every occasion and every person." T Queen enjoyed the tour too. " made us," she confided to the Canadian Prime Minister Mr Mackenzie King.

The tour was almost as famou for the few days the King and Queen spent in the United States, where they were the guests of President Franklin Roosevelt and his accomplishe wife Eleanor. The President's informal style was much appreciated by his guest, the modest, retiring King, and the personal letters to each other – "My dear President Roosevelt "My dear King George" – reflected the kindred spirits. Perhaps the most informal incident of the trip came wher after a private evening dinner and a long talk, the President suddenly said to the King: "Well, young man, it's time fo you to go to bed!"

Apart from the great personal success the King and Queen scored with the President, the triumphant reception accorded to them by the people of New York and the Atlantic seaboar surpassed all precedents. Geor III's descendant and his wife conquered the old colonies at the first attempt!

None of the Queen Mother's subsequent visits to Canada ev equalled the scale and sparkle the 1939 tour. But in 1954 she was back again, spending five days in Ottawa. Because of her visit she was unable to be in

...don for Prince Charles' sixth
...day, but he was thrilled to
...ive a transatlantic telephone
...from her instead. In June
... she went to Montreal to
...d the centenary
...brations of the Black Watch
...al Highland Regiment) of
...ada, of which she is
...onel-in-Chief, and three
...s later celebrated the jubilee
...e Toronto Scottish
...ment.
...ghtly more prolonged visit
...arranged in July 1967 when
...-day programme took her to

...Atlantic provinces of New
...nswick, Nova Scotia, Prince
...ward Island and
...vfoundland. In June 1974 she
...back again to present new
...ours to each of her two
...ments in Toronto and
...ntreal. Three years ago she
...a seven-day visit to Halifax
...Toronto and in July 1981
...nded the bicentennial
...brations of Niagara on the
...e during another 7-day visit
...Ontario. And in 1985 she
...back again, proclaiming
...her affection for Canada
...Canadians had not
...inished over the years.
...eight visits to Canada as
...en Mother and the Canadian
...nections she nurtures in
...ain have maintained the
...mitment engendered by that
...great tour when she herself
..., "When I'm in Canada, I
...a Canadian."

Prince Philip became President of World Wildlife Fund International in May 1981 and in February 1982 began one of what may become a series of crash courses to familiarise himself with conservation problems in all parts of the world. In a three-week tour

which he was serenaded (bottom right) during lunch by a local violinist.

(Below) In New Delhi Prince Philip presented the keys of two jeeps to the Asian Elephant Group at the Maurya Sheraton Hotel, after he had watched two audio visual shows detailing some of the World Wildlife Fund's Indian operations. Earlier that day he met the Prime Minister, Mrs Indira Gandhi (opposite page) and had lunch with her.

Prince Philip's 36-hour visit to Oman, where he was the guest of the Sultan (who paid a State Visit to Britain the following month) was arranged primarily to enable him to see the progress of one of the most exciting of all World Wildlife

which began on 17th February and took him to countries as far apart as Spain and Sri Lanka, he witnessed a wide range of activities from the minting of commemorative medals in Vienna to the reintroduction of captive oryx into the deserts of Oman.

In Austria he visited a compound (top right) at Haringsee where wild birds, including this ferocious-looking bearded vulture (opposite page top), are reared for research purposes, and a bird sanctuary (above right) at Marchegg, near the Czechoslovakian border. He had earlier been taken on a waggon ride round the Seewinkel to tour extensive wetlands populated with geese and other marsh birds, after

Fund's hundreds of projects. A decade ago the Arabian white oryx was almost extinct in the wild, a victim, like so many other species, of the trade in horn. The last few were rounded up and reared in a long-term programme of captivity and have only just been released back into the wild. The Duke arrived at the desert base at Yalooni, a two-hour helicopter journey from Muscat, to see how the oryx's reintroduction was progressing.

On arrival he met Dr and Mrs Mark Stanley-Price who run the project (bottom left) and was taken by landrover to where the oryx could be seen.

Unfortunately the previous night had brought a 1½" rainfall, the first rain for 5 years, and some of the Duke's wanderings on foot became a little hazardous (left). But he was able to see ten pure white oryx grazing placidly among acacia, eronbergiana and prosopis trees, and the project staff were particularly proud that one of the oryx had produced a healthy calf, now nine months old, which was adapting as well as the adults to its new environment. The Duke was fascinated to meet the local Bedou tribesmen (far left) who, armed with rifles, now have the job of protecting the herd from poachers.

On 7th March Prince Philip's tour took him to Port Sudan where the Sudanese Navy was

waiting to take him and World Wildlife Fund officials to a coral reef some twenty miles out to sea. The expedition had the advantage of the best weather of the tour, though the swell during the outward journey kept a few of the passengers fairly subdued. Even the Duke was on the point of succumbing towards the end, and on disembarking opted to climb the lighthouse *before* taking lunch! From the top of the lighthouse – "257 steps, if you're interested," he said on the way down – the brilliant variations in the sea's colour could be seen, while a walk along the jetty brought the sight

During his two-day visit to India, Prince Philip travelled from Jaipur to visit a tiger reserve at Sariska, about 150 miles south of New Delhi. On his arrival at the reserve headquarters tea was served in the garden and the layout of the reserve was explained (opposite page, bottom right) with details of the forty or so species of animals and birds which are known to inhabit it. A three-jeep convoy then left (centre pictures) for a fascinating two-hour journey deep into the reserve. There was

no risk of being met by tigers which come out only at night but a large variety of wildlife in evidence. Deer, neatly camouflaged in the dense woodland, were betrayed by shafts of sunlight filtering through, but showed little sign nervousness as the jeeps slow to allow their passengers a glimpse. The occasional jacka was spotted, blue-bull and rhesus monkeys abounded, th nests of weaver-birds dangled and swung from tall trees, and buzzards drifted high against

of brightly coloured fish, crabs and shoals of sardinellos in the rocky shallows (right). Prince Philip was taken by boat to look for fish in the deeper waters (above right) before returning to Port Sudan (centre and top left). From there he went to Suakin – almost a ghost town now since it literally fell to pieces thirty years ago or so – to record his visit to a small research centre (opposite page, bottom left).

y crags. On the way back the
[ve stopped at a look-out post
n which tourists (who were
admitted on this day) can
ch for tigers – but although
part of the visit was
nded into the early hours of
k, no tiger was sighted. On
return journey the stench of
ing meat heralded the quite
ping spectacle of a score of
zards tearing at the corpse of
e unfortunate animal, and
nting grisly morsels of
ping flesh in savage beaks.
this is no animal sanctuary,

is a problem the Germans will
have to sort out for themselves. I
am sure you can find a
compromise on this."
He went to Sri Lanka to see the
operation of a massive project
which involves the
reorganisation of whole
communities of elephants with
human populations and
industrial complexes to provide
the most efficient interplay
between the multiple needs of
each. He visited Sri Lanka's two
biggest sanctuaries – at Yale and
Wilpattu – and during a visit to

into the Parque Donana, a huge
– indeed Europe's largest –
wetland wildlife preserve, where
he spent most of the afternoon
and evening being driven from
habitat to habitat.
In Madrid there was a meeting
with his cousin King Juan Carlos
of Spain; and the affectionate
welcome given to him by Queen
Sophie made it obvious that
despite the fracas over the Royal
Wedding, the personal
relationships between the
English and Spanish royal
families were as strong as ever.

ept in that it is protected
m the ravages of man. The
elties of nature – as man
ght see it – are allowed their
urse in the interests of the
icate balance of life in the
d, and the fact was
compromisingly illustrated by
chance encounter with the
k reality.
e Duke's tour also took him
Egypt, where poor weather
ortunately put paid to a visit
n oasis in the Sinai and

limited his activities to a view of
the Giza Pyramids and, as he
somewhat bitterly put it, "a look
at Cairo's traffic."
An earlier leg of the tour found
the Duke in the midst of a
controversy in the province of
Schleswig-Holstein, in northern
Germany. Here the government
is proposing to build a six-mile
dyke across a nature reserve of
8400 acres, and ecologists are
convinced that the project will
threaten the natural uses to
which this marshland is put.
Hundreds of thousands of
migratory birds use it, millions
of sea birds find it a convenient
breeding ground, and it also
houses shallow-living sea life like
crabs and mussels.
The Duke had to tread gingerly
between the interests of the
administration, who were
concerned to prevent the loss of
life and property in the event of
a severe flood, and the ecologists
who feared the loss of wildlife
amenities. He achieved his
neutral stance with his usual
accomplishment. Speaking in
fluent German he said, "Both
interests are perfectly valid. This

a zoo in Colombo, he was
presented with a baby elephant,
named Geetha, which is now in
London Zoo.
He visited further projects in
Italy and Tunisia and finished
the entire tour with a 2-day visit
to Spain. Here he visited the
Gonzales Byass sherry bodegas
before joining a field trip at
Sanlucar de Barrameda near
Jerez. He enjoyed an open air
lunch before crossing the Rio
Guadalquivir by navy launch

Prince Philip returned to
Heathrow airport on 12th March
at the end of his three week tour,
during which it was announced
that he had been appointed
Vice-President of the
International Union for the
Conservation of Nature and
Natural Resources – the
scientific branch of the World
Wildlife Fund.

One of the most prestigious diplomatic events of February was the Ambassadorial Ball Soirée Française held on 22nd February at Grosvenor House in aid of the United Nations Association and UNICEF. This year's royal guest was the Duchess of Gloucester, sparkling as always in appearance and in form, seen (above and opposite page) as she arrived for the Soirée. The distinguished company included the patrons of honour – twenty five Ambassadors and High Commissioners – and another 25 patrons representing a vast range of national life – Margaret Duchess of Argyll and Lulu, Group-Captain Leonard Cheshire and Stirling Moss, Yehudi Menuhin and Esther Rantzen. Eric Morecambe, another patron, was there and the Duchess clearly enjoyed his company (top pictures). So much so that she may even have been tempted to appear in his next show!

The programme for the six-hour entertainment was superb. After the champagne reception, the guests were serenaded during a

ner of cream of cress soup,
food pancake, suprème de
aille and cherries with praline
cream. A fashion spectacular
the New Bond Street fashion
se Ungaro followed, before
nny Howard and his
chestra led the dancing until
midnight cabaret. A couple
affles were held, with
idays in Bali, India and
nisia as prizes in one, and
ellery, clothes and wines
tributing to a 13-part prize

in the other. For those with
ergy to spare there was a
cotheque until 2.00 in the
rning.
e Duchess left somewhat
lier than that but even so was
bably relieved that she had
engagements to fulfil the
owing day.

"The difference a year makes" had been a constant theme of comments about the Princess of Wales, who had by March 1982 not only been welcomed warmly and effusively into her role as third lady of the realm, but had also achieved that unbelievable degree of maturity which gave the impression that she was born to that position. One year, almost to the day, before these pictures were taken, Lady Diana Spencer made her first *coup de théâtre* at Goldsmiths Hall wearing a low-cut black taffeta evening dress which has since become almost legendary. Now, on 8th March 1982 she increased her tally of solo engagements when she paid an evening visit to the Victoria Palace Theatre in London to attend a special charity preview of the play "The Little Foxes."

For a solo engagement it had all the makings of a risky experience involving as it did Britain's most dazzling addition to the Royal Family for years – almost a folk heroine in her own right – and the legendary lady of the screen, known variously as the queen of Hollywood and the superstar of show business, Elizabeth Taylor. On top of that it was lost on no-one that Miss Taylor's leading role in "The Little Foxes" was her British stage début, and that the Princess of Wales was almost as much a novice in her role. So everyone was out to be on their best behaviour.

The Princess arrived attended by her senior lady in waiting, Anne Beckwith-Smith (opposite

page, left). Under her brilliant white fur jacket she was stunningly dressed in a long, white and champagne-coloured evening gown with puffed and gathered sleeves, glittering with sprays of sequins. Her much favoured low-cut neckline was set off by an ornate diamond necklace, and she looked happy and very fit and tanned after her recent Bahamian holiday. On her arrival she was presented with a bouquet and a toy fox (opposite page right) by 9-year-old

Caroline O'Neill: a moving moment, since her father, a police constable, was stabbed to death on duty 2 years before. The evening's show was in aid of the Metropolitan Police Benevolent Fund and the Army Benevolent Fund.

As guest of honour the Princess was introduced formally to the theatre management and the officials of the two charities, before being escorted to the Royal Box. Here she faltered, unsure as to when precisely to

move into the Box, so that while
the State Trumpeters began
their fanfare to greet her arrival
the spotlight fell on a cluster of
empty seats. Eventually, with
that apologetic blush which
disarms all critics, she made her
entry and, amid great applause,
took her seat.

The show went without a hitch.
Miss Taylor's performance left
audience and critics spellbound
and the play's producer Zev
Bufman said it was "the greatest
show she had put on."

"Something special," he called it.
The Princess thought it special
too: she applauded enthusias-
tically as the cast took several
curtain calls, and roared with
laughter when a Welsh
Guardsman went onto the stage
to present a bouquet to Miss
Taylor just as the curtain
descended upon him.

Afterwards the Princess met
members of the cast and realised
her long-held hope that she
would one day meet its leading
lady. Miss Taylor was in vivid
white, and the two of them
looked of equal rights. They
shook hands; the Princess said
how much she had enjoyed the
show and thanked her for "such
a lovely performance." When,
eventually, she had to go, she
made her way confidently to the
door and was applauded by the
cast as she did so. Miss Taylor
made as if to follow her,
imitating the same striding exit.
The Princess looked back: the
Queen of Hollywood was caught
in the act, and both burst out
laughing.

"The Princess was charming,
gracious and beautiful," Miss
Taylor said afterwards. "I was
more than thrilled to meet her."
For everyone, it seemed, the
evening was "something special."

Three generations of the Royal Family have been closely associated with what was originally called the Antique Dealers' Fair since its earliest days at Grosvenor House in the 1930's. Queen Mary, an inveterate gatherer of antiques, visited it as a matter of course – a fact evidenced by the inclusion in the 1982 exhibition of the ornate rosewood tea caddy which she bought there in 1937. The tea caddy now belongs to the Queen Mother, who as current Patron of the Fair, loaned it for the purpose. Today it is called the Burlington

House Fair, having moved to t[...] Royal Academy of Arts in Piccadilly in 1980. On 11th March 1982, Princess Margaret who last opened the Fair in 19[...] returned to open the most expansive and expensive of all its forty odd predecessors. Now

ommodated in ten galleries, nearly twice the size of the Fair, the 1982 exhibition a feast of superlatives. Sixty lers were offering for sale es worth more than £50 ion. Seventeen advisory mittees scrutinised every cle to guarantee authenticity.

There was everything from paintings to porcelain, glass and delicate silver to scientific instruments. The customary exhibition of loans, under the title "Connoisseurship & Collecting" displayed articles from the Queen's collection of paintings, the Duke and

Duchess of Kent's silverware, and Princess Alexandra's jewellery, as well as a gallery of pictures by Thomas Rowlandson, the 19th century artist who specialised in painting auction scenes.

Princess Margaret, who takes a close interest in the Fair from year to year, was fascinated by the display, and although her glasses may not become collector items in quite the same way, their appearance was rare enough to invite a certain amount of fascination too.

en Princess Anne married
tain Mark Phillips in
ember 1973 he took her,
their enviable South
erican honeymoon, to his
ried quarters, Oak Grove
se, at the Royal Military
demy Sandhurst. They didn't
there long, moving into
combe Park in 1977 just

ore Mark left the Army. As
lonel-in-Chief of three
iments it was probably only
atter of time before she was
ited back to her husband's
stamping ground and she
indeed accept an invitation
inspect the passing-out
ade of Academy graduates on
h March.
e parade was a comparatively
all one, only 89 student
cers taking part. They had
t graduated from Direct
urse No 19, after a twenty-

week training which began in
October 1981 and ended with
today's confirmed commissions.
The ceremonial which
surrounded the royal inspection
was predictable in character,
highly musical and spectacularly
enjoyable. A succession of
musical marches accompanied
the March-on Parade of Amiens
and Ypres Companies, before
the approach of Princess Anne
and her arrival at the reviewing
dais to the strains of the
National Anthem. During her
inspection (far left and centre
left) she drew a smile from one
bandsman, Sergeant Major
Gordon Saunders, whom she
recognised as having played for
her when she lived at Sandhurst
(top left). She returned to the
dais for the March Past (bottom
pictures) – a lengthy business
involving seven changes of
music, during which she found
time for chirpy conversation with
Colonel J E M Hughes, the
College Commander of Victory
College (opposite page).
Princess Anne made a short
closing address (opposite page
bottom right) remembering her
days at Sandhurst with affection,
and presented the Commander's
Medal to 2nd Lieutenant
Andrew Gregory, the best of his
course.
One newspaper called it the
"laughing-out" parade. It was
good to see Princess Anne,
whose relationships with the
Press are not always cordial,
thoroughly enjoying herself for
all to see.

Central London came tolerantly to a halt on the morning of 16th March as final preparations were completed for the first State Visit to Britain of His Majesty Sultan Qaboos bin Said Al Said of Oman. Persistent heavy rain in the early morning yielded before his arrival, but overcast skies made it certain that the processions from Victoria Station would be in closed carriages, as happened for the State Visit of the Nigerian President a year previously. Detachments of Household Cavalry (below) and massed

bands (left) paraded from barracks to route positions in capes and greatcoats, only the Kings Troop, Royal Horse Artillery (bottom left) sporting their resplendent gold braided uniforms as they rode towards Hyde Park to give the custom gun salutes.

The Sultan suffered his own experience of the British weather when his VC10 aircraft preparing to land at Gatwick, was struck on the nose cone by what was described as a severe bolt of lightning, which jolted the plane's passengers but otherwise did no harm. "I've heard of 21-gun salutes," said pilot, Denis Lowry, "but that was ridiculous." None the worse for his shock, the Sultan was greeted at Gatwick by the Duke of Gloucester and calmly emerged from the aircraft to join the Royal Train for Victoria. For many State Visitors to Britain, this habitual welcoming protocol is strange and novel,

but the Sultan would have understood it better than most. He has been a regular visitor – on semi-official as well as on several private occasions – to the country towards which he feels great affection. It was to Britain that he was sent at the age of 18 in 1958 to study privately in Suffolk before going to Sandhurst in 1960 and joining the 1st Battalion, the Cameronians, with BAOR in West Germany in 1962. It was with the aid of British officers that he overthrew his severely feudal father in 1970, after spending years in prison in Dhofar province, and the British came to his assistance three years later to put down an insurrection there, inspired by his Marxist neighbours in South Yemen (formerly British Aden). Sultan Qaboos, who owns a

ntry house in Berkshire,
s Britain and has immense
iration and respect for the
al Family.
welcoming by the Queen
Prince Philip at Victoria
ion (this page) was as much
rsonal greeting as a
ificant gesture in the history
e relations between Britain
Oman. As a token of his
sonal regard for the Queen,
Sultan had brought with him

Engineering of Clydebank
disclosed a £50 million order for
gas turbines for Oman's new
power station. For Prince Philip
(left) the welcoming ceremonies
at Victoria Station carried an
even more personal element,
since less than a month
previously he had been the
Sultan's guest during his short
trip to Oman as President of the
World Wildlife Fund.
Other members of the Royal

18ct gold insignia, studded
diamonds and rubies,
ich the makers, Spink and
s of London, ventured to
k was probably the richest of
kind anywhere in the world.
a token of the more practical
which the Sultan has in
ish technology, his visit
cided with the

announcement that he had
concluded a £215 million
contract with Cementation
International to build a
University in Oman, with the
possible benefit of ancillary
equipment and services worth
£140 million to be provided by
British firms, and before the end
of the visit, John Brown

Family were also there to greet
the Sultan – amongst them
Princess Anne and Captain
Mark Phillips (overleaf with
the Duchess of Gloucester) and
the Duke and Duchess of Kent
(bottom right). There was a
slight hitch in the welcoming
ceremonies when it was
discovered that Baroness
Phillips, the Lord Lieutenant of
London – who was supposed to
introduce the Sultan to the
Prime Minister – had not
arrived. Apparently her newly-
employed chauffeur failed to
collect her from home. But
protocol notwithstanding, the

Prime Minister, along with her Cabinet colleagues Foreign Secretary Lord Carrington and Home Secretary Mr William Whitelaw (below right), were duly introduced. They met again the following day at Downing Street, where Mrs Thatcher entertained the Sultan to lunch, and had "extremely friendly and cordial talks."

The journey from Victoria Station, preceded by the Sultan's inspection of the Guard of Honour, was not without incident. Just as the Queen and her guest, with Prince Philip, were leaving in the Irish State Coach, a brown Renault 16 was spotted parked in the Mall between Clarence House and Buckingham Palace. Suspecting the worst, police quickly flashed a message to the procession organisers to detour through Birdcage Walk while the car was detonated by a small controlled

The Sultan's afternoon programme followed the usual pattern – an address of welcom by the Lord Mayor of Westminster at St. James's Palace, a courtesy visit to the Queen Mother at Clarence House, and a visit to Westminster Abbey to lay a wreath on the grave of the Unknown Warrior. That evenir the Queen gave a State Banqu at Buckingham Palace which th whole of the Royal Family, sav Prince Andrew, Prince Edward Princess Alice and Princess Alexandra and her husband, attended. In her speech the Queen admitted that Britain ha

explosion – which revealed that it was harmless. Its owner, Michael Waterfield of Canterbury, had parked it there without realising what concern it would cause, and he later commemorated the fact by insisting that the dent in his boot, caused by the detonation, should not be knocked out. Meanwhile, however, thousands of people, many Omanis included, who had waited in the Mall for a glimpse of the royal visitor, were disappointed.

criticised for losing interest
the Arabian peninsula but
...nised that "we shall keep
...with Oman."

...r visiting the Prime Minister
...following day, Sultan Qaboos
...guest of honour at the Lord
...or's luncheon at the
...dhall, at which the Duke of
...t was present. It was here
...the Sultan made his most
...tly political speech of the
...re visit, condemning "Soviet
...erialist interference in the
... World" which "exploits the
...tion for its own ends." He
...d a peaceful solution to the
...stinian problem on the basis
...n honourable settlement of
...plight of the Palestinians "in
...interests of justice and
...mon humanity" and was
...vinced that our friends in
...West have an important
...onsibility...in solving the
...lems that confront the
...dle East today."

...sidering how vulnerable
...an is in an area of seething
...rnational politics and vital
...mercial importance to the
...d economy, his words were
...-implacable against
...ntial enemies and logically
...ctive towards friends. For in
...tion to the mainland of
...an, the Sultan rules a small
...gle of land just to the north

Bovington Camp in Dorset to
see a display of British military
hardware in action. The Royal
Armoured Corps put on a
superlative demonstration of
tanks and artillery, sufficiently
impressing the Sultan for him to
order £35 million of Chieftain
tanks for use in his own national
army. On his return to London,
he returned the Queen's
hospitality by giving a State
Banquet for her and other
members of the Royal Family at
Claridges. Fewer members of
her family attended than at the
Buckingham Palace Banquet
two days before, but Princess
Margaret (top and opposite

...t of the United Arab
...irates, which controls the
...its of Hormuz through
...ch every oil tanker must pass
...n the Persian Gulf. He
...fidently promised his
...dhall hosts that all the
...stern World's oil which sails
...ugh the Straits to keep their
...nomies alive, would continue
...lo so, and paid tribute to the
...tribution that Britain had
...de towards bringing Oman
... of the backward state in
...ch he had inherited it in

1970. In those days there was
hardly a metalled road in the
whole country. Now it fairly
bristles with beautifully tarmac'd
desert roads, airports, schools,
clinics, factories, electricity
systems and television. And in
the forces, the process of
Omanisation – the gradual
handover of knowhow and
leadership from the invited
British forces to the Omanis –
has taken its first tentative steps.
The last full day of the Sultan's
visit was taken up by a visit to

page left) and the Duchess of
Gloucester (right) enhanced the
occasion with their richly
coloured evening gowns and
sparkling jewellery. As did the
Queen, who was delighted to be
welcomed personally by the
Sultan in this colourful finale to
a most satisfactory visit.
The British Royal Family's
amicable personal relations with
Oman's Sultan has parallels with
other tribal or hereditary rulers.
Perhaps the best example is the
Nepalese monarchy whose

present head King Birendra is a close personal friend of Prince Charles. The Prince, with his great-uncle Lord Mountbatten attended the King's coronation at Katmandu in 1975, and visited the King during his solo tour in December 1980. The Duke and Duchess of Gloucester spent a fortnight or so in Nepal in February 1982, and the Queen and Duke of Edinburgh paid their second

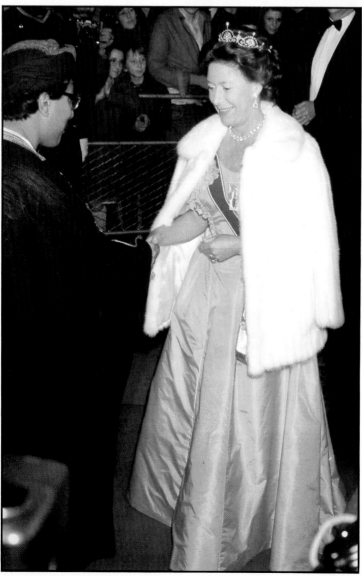

e Visit to the mountain
dom, on their way to
ralia and New Zealand
r in 1986 – almost
ly a quarter of a
ury after their first
there as part of a six-
k tour of the East in

Over a century and a half ago Britain negotiated the Peace of Nanking with Imperial China after a comparatively brief skirmish over the opium trade. The terms were favourable to Britain: reparations of £5¾ million, the opening of five Chinese ports to British trade, and the cession of Hong Kong. Immediately, the Royal Navy recruited Hong Kong sailors into her ships and once in Britain many of them eventually settled in the great bustling, north-western port of Liverpool. The descendants of some of those Chinese recruits were presented on 2nd April 1982 to the Prince and Princess of Wales, who arrived in their maroon Rolls-Royce to perform the official opening of the Pagoda of the Hundred Harmonies on the outskirts of the City's Chinese quarter. It isn't really a pagoda at all, but its design imitates the style as closely as the purpose of the building allows. And the purpose is, quite simply, a community centre, specifically for the oldest Chinese community of its kind in Western Europe, and the second largest, next to London's Soho, in Britain. The Merseyside Chinese thus became the first in Europe to have their very own community building. So the day was one of special pride for them.

There is no getting away from the fact that Merseyside's social history this century has been a tough one. Its communities have been stricken with some of the worst effects of unemployment and poverty when times have been bad, and popular impatience with Central Government has boiled over into violence and disorder: the "Scuffers" strike of 1920, the Depression of the 1920's and 1930's, a whole series of debilitating dock strikes, and more recently the street riots in Toxteth, born, it was thought, out of racial tension and bitterness. But today the mood had changed and the thousands present were out to have a good

before," pulled her towards him and planted a decisive kiss on her cheek, momentarily giving her quite a shock. For her part the Princess made three-year-old Colin Griffiths' day when he slipped between the legs of Special Branch police officers and ran towards her to present his 70p worth of yellow tulips. He turned back towards his mother, then changed his mind and made for the Princess, said "I love you" and smothered her with kisses. As she bent down to hug him, the crowd cheered them both on, thrilled by the spontaneity of it all. "I'm not

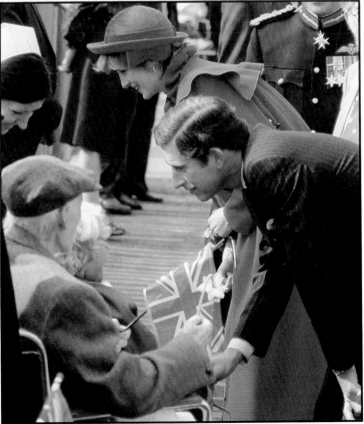

ryone seemed to enter into spirit of elation, including Prince and Princess, who e at their most delightfully rmal. Prince Charles ched as his wife received a line of VIPs in the coming ceremony, and ded to join the back of the ue. When his turn came he , "I believe we've met

really surprised at what he did," said his mother afterwards. "He really adores her. She's his favourite person and he loves to watch her on television."
The opening ceremony was typically spectacular. The Prince and Princess each painted-in the eyes of the hundredweight-and-a-half ceramic dragon at the entrance to the building in the

ner of the New Year
vities, when the dragon
es to life. The pagoda's
gon in fact had electric light
s for eyes, giving the
ding a glowing identity at
t.

royal couple toured the
re and saw the Chinese
ription on the outer wall
ling: "This community will
e for prosperity, harmony
the aspiration for future
ti-racial integration and
erstanding with all peoples."
nembering Toxteth, they
e noble sentiments.

centre itself realised an
ration – that of Mr Brian
Sheng Wang, who at only 32
full-time Community Liaison
cer and who in the seven
s since he arrived from
van has devoted his time to
ting the circumstances in
ch young Chinese might
ain educational and career
ortunities. His efforts have
ed him in high regard: he
much to secure the £¼
ion needed for the centre –
8,000 from the Inner
Partnership, the remainder
n local fund-raising events.
Prince and Princess were
rtained to an eight-course
ch prepared by cooks from
of Liverpool's Chinese
aurants. It lived up to the
utation of all Chinese meals:
e were spare ribs, crispy
fed phoenix-tail prawns with
ng onions, fried duckling
jasmin, sweet and sour fish,
ken in yellow bean sauce
platters of fruits offered by
t were mysteriously referred
s "celestial ladies." Over
ch, and during the folk
cing display that
mpanied it, the Princess
ke to Mr Wang's 30-year-old
Nora. As luck would have it
too was expecting a baby – a
nth earlier than the Princess
there was plenty to talk
ut. But Mrs Wang remained
rutable afterwards: "We
ed quite a lot about the sort
ning that ladies like us do
about." So evidently did
ce Charles. He told Mrs
istine Cheetham and Mrs Jill
ker, both also pregnant: "It
st be something in the
er." Surely he must know
er than that!

On 13th April, the Tuesday after Easter, Queen Elizabeth the Queen Mother left Clarence House for the Royal Albert Hall to attend a gala concert which, according to an understatement in the programme notes, Philharmonic Orchestra, with whom he was to sing, and the Queen Mother's presence as Patron of the Orchestra at a concert staged as part of its National Appeal made the evening one of superlatives.

promised "to be one of London's musical events of the year." It was in fact the only scheduled appearance at a concert in the United Kingdom in 1982 of that superlative tenor opera singer Luciano Pavarotti. The occasion was all the more special because Pavarotti himself had substantially reduced his fees to help the Royal

Indeed, when a recording of th concert was shown on televisio a few days later, it was on the cards that opera had recruited substantial number of new admirers.

At 47, Pavarotti had acquired every tribute the opera world could possibly heap on one man. For a singer whose professional début did not occ until the age of 26, it must be praise indeed to be commende for having a voice which in various ways can be likened to Caruso's, Gigli's or Björling's. He first performed in England 1962 – at Covent Garden, whic occupies a very important plac in the milestone history of his career.

The programme was by mode standards a colossal one, with four orchestral pieces and seve operatic arias including three b Verdi and two by Puccini, and after the concert Pavarotti was introduced to the Queen Moth (above left). Opera is not thought to be the Queen Mother's listening forte though she has had an accomplished e for music since childhood, and when young sang "very prettily according to her music mistres But it is inconceivable that Pavarotti's performance did les than rivet her – these pictures show her looking as fresh as a daisy, lively and with that famo wagging finger (opposite page

om left) in animated
versation with the celebrity
ose singing she unreservedly
oyed. For a great-
ndmother striding confidently
ards her 82nd birthday, she
ked a picture of appreciation,
charmed by Pavarotti's
alrous gestures –
iniscent of some Renaissance

established and she may have
passed a few tips on.
Financially the concert was a
massive success, and the Royal
Philharmonic will have been
pleased and thankful for that.
The box office takings showed
the largest amount their
performances had ever drawn at
any concert hall anywhere in the

world – almost £150,000. For an
organisation which at some of its
concerts pays back to the
Government in VAT more than it
receives in grants, that must be
compensation enough, but it was
also satisfying to know that this
was not an occasion solely for
the wealthy. Of the 6,000 tickets
sold, 3,500 were available at £15
or less, including 1,000 student
tickets at only £2.50 each. The
result was the largest "live"
audience ever to hear Pavarotti
in the UK, and every one of
them, like the Queen Mother,
surely satisfied with the exquisite
performance of a man who
according to the title of one of
his own records is "King of the
High C's."

lant (far right), and as
illed as Pavarotti was
noured by the presentation to
of one of his eight records
rently available (above right).
d did they, perhaps for a few
ef moments, exchange the
est gossip on the equestrian
ne? Pavarotti's interest in
se racing and thoroughbred
eding is as recent as the
een Mother's is well

The thirty-first Badminton Three-day Event – it has been held every year since its inauguration in 1949 – got underway in the grounds of the late Duke of Beaufort's Gloucestershire mansion on 15th April. This prestigious, well-attended and thorough test of all-round horsemanship, with the Whitbread Trophy and a prize of £3,000 for the winner, attracted a gate of almost 200,000 people, and a field of seventy-nine competitors. Among them were twenty initiates aged less than 25, as well as the much more seasoned campaigners, Princess Anne (below) and her husband Captain Mark Phillips (right).

sadly, he ultimately attended only as a spectator.

The dressage took up two day of the Badminton programme and both Princess Anne (No 7 and Captain Phillips (No 83) competed on the second day. Both had submitted their hors to the usual veterinary inspection on the evening of th 14th April, and each horse was declared sound. But despite th and the previous day's practice runs (below and right), Captain Phillips' mount Classic Lines conceded 60.6 dressage penalty points and left him down the field. Princess Anne, who had not competed at Badminton since 1979, fared rather better with a

Princess Anne (seen above riding the Queen's horse Stevie B in the first phase of the competition, the dressage, on 16th April) has never yet won at Badminton, but Captain Phillips, like Lucinda Prior-Palmer-Green who won in 1973, 1976, 1977 and 1979, has run out victor on a record four different occasions – in 1971 and 1972 on

his horse Great Ovation, in 1974 on the Queen's horse Columbus, and in 1981 on Lincoln, a horse sponsored by Range Rover Team, as part of the deal he made with Land Rover Ltd in 1980. The sponsorship, arranged amid fierce public criticism, brought Captain Phillips more than £75,000 in two years, including over £10,000 in prize

money – mostly from his tally of sixteen victories in 1981. Shortly before Badminton it was announced that the sponsoring partnership would be continued until December 1983, with an option to extend for two further years. This took Captain Phillips into the reckoning for the 1984 Olympics at Los Angeles, an event at which,

final total of 58.2 penalties. The following day, fortunes wer quite dramatically reversed. Captain Phillips, who later declared that he was "thrilled with Classic Lines' performance in the dressage and cross-country," came home with a clear round in the cross country phase – recognised as one of th most gruelling of its kind in

Europe, with its total of 32 obstacles comprising steps, ditches, hedges, rails, fences, ski-jumps and lakes. This performance lifted him to eventual 14th place, two places short of the entitlement to the smallest prize of £125. Princess Anne did not, however, have such a good day. She had already had one of her regular altercations with the army of photographers who have followed her equestrian career with unstinting interest, when her exasperation reached breaking point the previous day. "Why don't you all grow up," she told them. "You've been taking the same pictures of me every day for three days. Why

don't you naff off. Go on, shove off." In no mood to do either, the photographers were waiting for her at the eighteenth fence in the cross country – the upturned punt barring entry into the lake. This is usually the spot where her husband comes a cropper, but this time Stevie B's hooves clipped the punt and Princess

for them both. In June 1981 Mark had been in the winning British team at the European championships at Hooge Mierde in Holland and was joined by Princess Anne at the Burghley Horse Trials in September – she won there in 1971 to take the European Championship that year. Unfortunately both of them landed in water ditches during the cross country, and came away unplaced.

October was another bad month: although Captain Phillips won £1,500 prize money at Wylye Horse Trials near Salisbury, Princess Anne was nearly knocked down by another rider when she was helping to rebuild one of the fallen fences. Later that month Mark went to

ne, unable to control his balance, nosedived with him o the lake (opposite page). e retrieved the horse and ddled out of the lake, her ite nylon breeches nsparent and her riding boots of water. Surprisingly eerful – or at least philosophi-(top right) – she decided to

retire from the event and trotted off back to the stables, though not before she had cast a final malediction the way of the photographers. "I hope you're all happy. You've got what you wanted now."

So ended the Phillipses twelfth Badminton challenge, in what had been a busy equestrian year

compete in Australia, where he found considerably more interest being shown in the rumours of a rift in his marriage. In a radio interview, for which he was said to have asked a fee of £6,000, he faced up to the long-running stories of a liaison between him and former BBC newsreader Angela Rippon, who had been commissioned to write a book called "Mark Phillips, The Man and His Horses" – which, incidentally she launched at Badminton on 15th April. He denied any romance, saying that he and Princess Anne had got to know Miss Rippon very well – "after all, it takes a long time to write a book. Princess Anne and

I are not at all happy about the rumours. Nor was Miss Rippon – she too is happily married." The same month brought an astonishing statement from Councillor Jim Spencer, a Liberal member of Otley Town Council in West Yorkshire who, in a debate about the local horse-riding fraternity, protested that "horses are ridden by base and coarse people like Princess Anne." Just a joke, he said afterwards.
Captain Phillips' luck failed to improve over the New Year. He had to admit that he needed a complete break from horses after a heavy 18-month

schedule. He had taken an enforced rest when his back began to play up in November, and decided to prolong it over Christmas. He then found himself a stone and a half overweight as his training deadline approached and had to work hard to get himself in trim again.
In January he was unable to get from Gatcombe to Upminster where he was due to compete in the Martell Cognac Championships; heavy snow delayed his train from Stroud, and attempts to charter a helicopter failed. By February he was campaigning to save Aintree, now in one of its recurring death throes; he had jumped the course back in 1979 and thought it "one of the greatest experiences of my life: it would be a tragic loss."
March saw both him and Princess Anne back in the saddle with a vengeance: at Crookham Horse Trials he rode his "second" horse Blizzard II,

while she competed on her younger horse Soul Song. They both competed later at Downlands Horse Trials near Liphook, and Mark was out again at Wendover Horse Trials towards the end of the month. And, as a postscript to Badminton, Princess Anne rode Soul Song at Hagley Horse Trials in Worcestershire in April. He refused at the water ditch, and she fell in. Plus ça change …
Princess Anne has long been branded the black sheep of the Royal Family, and often without the tolerant endearments which that expression often connotes.

Her frequent brushes with the Press – usually at some equestrian event – and the Press' own retaliatory sarcasm against her whenever she uses the word "one" to mean "I" or "me," has brought the Princess' public image into what at one stage looked like irretrievable disfavour.

One accusation frequently levelled against her is that sh unnecessarily distances herse from the Press and her publ Yet she is the best known of the Queen's children in the sense that she has invited a considerable amount of publ into her activities both publi and private. Ever since the

rather disastrous pre-weddin interview she and Captain Phillips gave in November 1 for transmission by both television corporations – "It a night to turn monarchists ir republicans and republicans monarchists," said one critic interviews and filming faciliti have been given regularly in around Oak Grove House at Sandhurst, and Gatcombe P; As a result, we have enjoyed particular a unique insight in the way the Princess and her husband throw themselves ir their consuming equestrian pastimes.

the '80s, Princess Anne
y spoke of her public life
w she approaches it, how
ortant she feels it is, what
gets out of it. That was
y remedied when she was
viewed in December 1981
e ITV programme
ncess Anne, Her Working
' In it she envisaged that her

iren would be free to pursue
careers without having to
orm official duties. She cited
cess Margaret's children as
nples, but she might more
y have chosen the family of
great-aunt, the late Princess
al. Her brothers produced
ilies who answered the royal
but her own sons, Lord
ewood and Mr Gerald
elles, are conveniently off
royal hook.
to demonstrate that he has
ntention of being very royal,
cess Anne's son Peter ran
k at Badminton, giving the
ds more entertainment than
had paid to see. Finding a

kindred spirit in 10-year-old
Alexander Lochore, whose
father is a friend of Princess
Anne, he began racing round
the collecting ring, squealing and
shouting as he darted between
his mother's legs, swinging
round them and throwing both
parents off balance with some
pretty physical charges. Captain

Phillips remonstrated (opposite
page right), so did Princess
Anne, but Peter was in too
boisterous a mood to take the
hint. Eventually, Princess Anne
took him off (above) to one of
her grooms and he was led,
protesting, out of the
compound.

Two of the most recent royal regulars at Badminton are Prince Michael and Princess Michael of Kent, seen here on 17th April enjoying the thrills and spills of the cross country Speed and Endurance Test, as well as a few much more personal moments (bottom picture and opposite page extreme right). Their attendance each year (including 1981, only days before the Princess gave birth to her second child) is no mere social appearance. Both share wide equestrian interests. Prince Michael often goes hunting, though not always with satisfactory results: in October 1981 he was one of a succession of riders who were thrown from their horses at a Meet of the Quorn in Leicestershire. Princess Michael, a keen huntswoman too, supports equestrian events close to her home at Nether Lyppiatt, competes in horse trials and point-to-points, and is rated highly enough to have made the front page of *Horse and Hound*.

to the Solent for Cowes Week, and took both him and his wife to Rhode Island in 1983 to support the British entry *Victory* in the America's Cup. At the other extreme of their combined interests is their penchant for the arts. Like her talented mother-in-law, Princess Marina, Princess Michael paints, though "very badly" she admits, "in water colours," preferring to

1982. Starring Jeremy Irons, it was one of three official British entries that year and Prince Michael backed it financially. Among the films and plays Prince and Princess Michael saw in the same year were "The Little Foxes" in March, when they met Elizabeth Taylor; the charity premiere of

The horse world forms only part of the royal couple's sporting interests. Despite the accident sixteen years ago which almost killed him, Prince Michael has never lost his enthusiasm for bobsleighing. As President of the British Bobsleigh Association he agreed to open the Thorpe Training Run for bobsleigh practice in Chertsey in September 1981, and the following January visited the British team at St Moritz as they trained for their annual assault on the World Championships. Prince Michael's interest in sailing takes him frequently

paint still lifes and flowers: "I don't paint as well as Princess Marina did and feel I have a lot to live up to." Her ambition is to have one of her works accepted by the Society of Women Artists, whose annual exhibition she opened at the Mall Galleries in February.

The cinema and theatre have Prince Michael's support: he visited the Cannes Film Festival to follow the fortunes of the film "Moonlighting" in May

"On Golden Pond" at the Empire Leicester Square, and the new £1½ million production of "The Pirates of Penzance" at the Savoy.

Rumour had it that the Prince and Princess could even be going into television, with Prince Michael as non-executive director of the television company AMTV and his wife as a breakfast television presenter. But it proved a false hope: he is kept busy enough with

interests in the City;
has probably had her fill
e media, and has anyway
trying for five years to
her book on Elizabeth
ohemia – the Winter
en, daughter of our own
James I and a direct
stress of the House of
dsor.
as during a visit to Holland
search the book that, in
uary 1982, the Princess
taken ill with severe
ominal pains. She was
ed off to King Edward VII
pital for Officers in
ylebone, where two days of

catch up on her work. And
work, which over the years
has taken her and Prince
Michael from their London
residence, Kensington Palace,
to as far afield as Belize,
to represent the Queen at
independence in 1981, seems
to be colourful, varied,
interesting and enjoyable.
Certainly few have taken up the
royal role with as much
unashamed gusto as has
Princess Michael, with her regal
bearing, superbly chosen
wardrobe, glittering jewels and
expansive gestures. David
Bailey's official photograph of

mination and tests amid
ours that she was pregnant
ad suffered a miscarriage,
wed that her gall bladder was
cause of the trouble. Prince
hael was at her bedside for
st of this worrying time, and
brought their two children
ee their mother who "was
sing them, and the doctors
ught it would be a tonic for
' Lord Frederick looked a
ure in his piped jacket and
ckerbockers. After an
ration for the removal of her
bladder, Princess Michael
erged from hospital "feeling
" on 1st March, and went
k to Kensington Palace to

her in a rich blue gown with
extravagant ruffles and puffed
sleeves was a classic of royal
portraiture, and the image of
one who revels in her new role
was well captured.
Unfortunately the Princess is
not without her critics, as the
sensations in 1985 over her
father's wartime role in the
SS, and her alleged affair with
an American millionaire, so
disastrously proved. Those
stories and their aftermath may
have reduced her faith in human
charity, but she is strong
enough to be able to continue
to develop her life in her own
enthusiastic way.

The Queen's absence from Badminton was only her second since the event began, the last time being after the birth of Prince Edward in 1964. It was ironic that after more than half a century's wrangling over the most effective and acceptable way to sever the last colonial link between Britain and Canada, the formal ceremony to despatch the quarrel should have been so hastily organised that the Queen's constitutional presence in Canada should be necessary on the very dates of the one country event she has so loyally

attended since before her accession.

The Duke of Beaufort was naturally very disappointed – so the Duchess confirmed, adding, "and I know the Queen is too." Colonel Frank Weldon, Director of the Horse Trials, went one better and disclosed that the Queen, whose job in Canada he called "dreary and unpleasant," had written to the Duke, regretting her absence, saying that she would have liked the Canadian ceremony to have been postponed till after Badminton and that she had tried to get the dates changed so that she could attend both. An almighty row broke out in the Badminton camp over the Colonel's revelation, while Buckingham Palace tried to keep a delicate neutrality.

It was nothing like the row that awaited the Queen when she arrived in Ottawa (above right), having travelled in a Canadian Armed Forces Boeing 707 (top right) from Heathrow on 15th April. (Unusually, she stepped out of the aircraft in the same outfit as she had entered it. She usually changes en route). For as she was being introduced by Governor-General Ed Schreyer (above, far right) to a line of dignitaries, inspecting the guard of honour (opposite page, left centre) and signing the VIP's Visitors Book (opposite page

bottom left), the Premier of t separatist Quebec provincial government, René Levesque, was finalising plans for half a dozen protest meetings, and a boycott of the official ceremon at which Canada would assum full responsibility for her own constitution. Monsieur Levesque, the man who achieved fleeting notoriety a f years back for holding a lighte cigarette as the Queen was be officially introduced to him, sa "It's crazy for the Queen to come here. We refuse to acce her bringing us our symbolic

pendence," and his political
nsigence on this occasion
partly responsible for the
sive security which
ounded the Queen during
visit.

issue which prompted the
en's visit has loomed large in
ada's history. Anti-colonial
llions in Canada in 1837 had
thirty years later, to the
sh North America Act,
h placed the internal affairs
e Canadian confederation of
inces within their own
er, while constitutional and
gn affairs were reserved to

Great Britain. A gentle process
of transferring these reserved
powers followed, and by the
time of the Imperial Conference
of 1926 only constitutional
sovereignty remained seriously
at issue. By the Statute of
Westminster of 1931, the British
Parliament lost the power to
make any legislation on behalf·
of Canada, or indeed of any
other Dominion. Formal
approval by Britain of Canadian
laws amending its constitution
was retained, and it was this
which proved a sticking point,
not so much between Canada

and embittered Eskimos whose
claims, if they went unrecognised
or merely ignored, might swell
the ranks of the disaffected.
Though at no time during the
Queen's four-day visit could
these considerations have been
far from her mind, she looked
her usual composed and
welcoming self as, on 16th April,
she entertained guests at a State
reception and banquet at the
Governor-General's residence
(overleaf). Prince Philip,
who had been unable to travel
with her the previous day
because of an official

and Britain but between the
English and French-speaking
populations of Canada.
Although, under the new
Constitution Act of 1982, all
restrictions, whether substantive
or merely formal, on the rights
of Canadians to legislate for
themselves were removed, the
substitution of the new charter
of rights, both human and
political, was seen by the
separatists as giving perpetual
power to the English-speaking
majority. Monsieur Levesque
had secured the support of
dispossessed Canadian Indians

engagement in Berkshire – taking the Salute at a passing out parade of REME Officers at the Princess Marina College, Berkshire – arrived in Ottawa in time to join her for this occasion (left and above left). The Queen was wearing the shimmering, lattice-patterned evening dress she had worn the previous month at the State banquet she gave at Buckingham Palace for the Sultan of Oman, with her Canadian orders in place of her more usual personal family orders. She also sported a matching combination of diamond and ruby jewellery – the necklace which she has worn on State occasions since her State Visit to Western Germany in 1965 and the tiara which she had had made up from her own collection of stones for the visit to Windsor by the President of Mexico in 1973, and which has been her particular favourite on previous visits to Canada. Beneath portraits of previous

Governors-General of Canada, the Queen and Prince Philip, accompanied by the present Governor-General and his wife (bottom left), welcomed a long succession of official and diplomatic guests, among whom was the British Shadow Foreign Minister, former Prime Minister Edinburgh's Award. A hundred young achievers were accordingly presented at Rideau Hall on 16th April. The following day the Queen presided at the swearing-in of eleven new members of the Privy Council – including all the provincial premiers save intact, while the Commons and Senate chambers were completely rebuilt in the more austere, less florid style of post-War years. And that evening, her last of the visit, she attended a gala concert at the National Arts Centre as well as a dinner given in her honour by the Canadian Prime Minister, Pierre Trudeau (opposite page, below right and bottom pictures).

The central ceremony of the visit and the signing of the Proclamation giving effect to the new Act, took place in weather as variable as its political fortunes in the decades before

Mr James Callaghan (top right).
The banquet was one of several official engagements which kept the Queen and Prince Philip well occupied throughout their stay in Canada as part of the ceremonial ancillary to the handing over of the country's constitution. Prince Philip had already attended one of his frequent receptions at which he awards Certificates of Achievement to winners at Gold Standard of the Duke of Monsieur Levesque – in a ceremony in the Privy Council chamber of the Canadian Parliament.
She also inaugurated the East Block of the legislative complex, newly renovated in a four-year-long project, in keeping with the original mid-Victorian character of the building as a whole – the West Block has been changed substantially through the years, and the Centre Block was destroyed by fire in 1916, leaving only the Parliamentary Library

ate agreement on 5th
ember 1981. As if to
hesy an age of uncertainty,
ant sunshine alternated with
endously heavy downpours
in as the Royal Standard
e over the rambling, Gothic
ament building and fluttered
y atop the 220 foot high
e Tower. A crowd of 50,000
d on and around the vast
s in front of it, unfurling
rellas or hastily putting on
aks and cagoules, while 24
on people watching
ision more comfortably at
e awaited the arrival of the
en.
re was little in the way of
minary activity. In the space
a hour before the official
mony, a succession of
nguished guests arrived at
Parliament building, while

the waiting crowds were
entertained by a programme of
music and song from the Mount
Royal Children's Choir from
Calgary, "Les Alino" from
Moncton, New Brunswick and
the Central Band of the
Canadian Forces. Ultimately, ten
minutes before the Queen, Mr
Trudeau arrived, smiling with
the satisfaction of achievement
but conscious of the significance
of the solemn and historic
occasion to follow, and was
greeted by Canada's Secretary of
State. Five minutes later the
Governor-General arrived and
proceeded to the saluting base
to receive an official vice-regal
salute and to greet the Queen.
She and Prince Philip arrived at
Parliament Hill in a hundred-
year-old State Landau drawn by
four black horses, and escorted

by 47 scarlet-jacketed officers of the Royal Canadian Mounted Police, also on shining black horses. The Queen wore a blue woollen coat and matching hat and, for the ceremony itself, added two of her Canadian orders. Prince Philip looked dapper and impressive, as usual on such occasions, if less familiar in the uniform of the Royal Canadian Regiment of which he is Colonel. As they alighted from their carriage, a 21-gun salute, fired by the 30th Canadian Field Regiment, boomed from across the Ottawa River, while the band of the Royal 22nd Regiment, comprising mostly French-speaking soldiers, struck up with the National Anthem. Overhead a noisy but impressive flypast by two squadrons of the Canadian Air Force completed the ceremonial salute as the Queen began a short inspection of the Guard of Honour provided by the Royal 22nd Regiment's 3rd Battalion. This completed, its band played the Canadian anthem "O Canada"

sovereignty." He was anxious to lay none of the blame for the decades-long delay at Britain's feet and willingly acknowledged that the rump of the British connection had lasted so unconscionably long for no better reason than that no-one could agree how best to have the last vestiges of power transferred

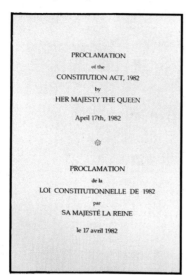

PROCLAMATION
of the
CONSTITUTION ACT, 1982
by
HER MAJESTY THE QUEEN

April 17th, 1982

PROCLAMATION
de la
LOI CONSTITUTIONNELLE DE 1982
par
SA MAJESTÉ LA REINE

le 17 avril 1982

and the crowds momentarily fell emotionally silent. But not for long. To frantic cheers from crowds up to ten deep in places, the royal couple were led by Mr Trudeau to a specially constructed dais (seen above right), ablaze with red carpet and plush thrones, for the open-air signing ceremony.
In a brief foreword, the Secretary of State explained the ceremony, its background, its purpose and its procedure. Mr Trudeau then stood to deliver his own address, rejoicing, though respectfully that "The Constitution has at last come home," and that "Today at long last, Canada has acquired full and complete

Minister, and the Registrar General of Canada, it was brought, as carefully as if it were the Dead Sea Scrolls, to a lectern as the Queen returned to her Throne, and its contents were read aloud, for all to hear, by the Under-Secretary of State, Mrs Huguette Labelle. The last

Canadian hands. "This is ast colonial link with in," he continued; "the end ong winter, the breaking up e ice-jams and the nning of a new Spring."

Proclamation putting the measure into effect was brought to the Queen who, her Canadian Prime ister, proceeded to a shed table for the signing mony. She was the first to her pen to it, signing abeth R' in a script so sually large for her that

historians might have been reminded of John Hancock, who signed his name to the American Declaration of Independence deliberately grandly, so that, as he said, "King George can read it without having to put on his spectacles."
After the document had been additionally signed by the Prime

word lay with the Queen. There was a nine-jet fly-past from the Canadian Armed Forces' precision squadron 'The Snowbirds,' but the noise they made was nothing to the enormous thunderclap which coincided with the Queen's first words and preceded another torrential helping of rain. The Queen ventured no interpretation of this celestial signal, in jest or otherwise, but

spoke, in oblique references to the separatists, about the "differences and rivalries which have been part of Canada's history, and will probably always exist in such a vast and vigorous land." More specifically, she continued: "Although we regret the absence of its Premier, it is right to associate the people of Quebec with this celebration, because without them Canada would not be what she it today." So Great Britain's last hold on Canada's independence had been yielded up with good grace, and the old Dominion's "new Spring" had begun joyfully. And still the rain came down. It continued throughout the royal walkabout, in which the Queen held her own large black umbrella as she met a few of the enormous crowd of spectators, many of whom carried banners proclaiming 'God Save Canada,' or 'Proud to be Canadian' or 'Long Live the Queen . . . and Trudeau Too.' Meanwhile, the resilient Monsieur Levesque

ched with considerable
sfaction the progress of his
protest rallies in Montreal.
,000 audience, somewhat
r than expected, but
able enough considering the
ther, turned up in Jeanne
ce Park, waving anti-royalist
ners, protesting about the
ence of a 'foreign monarch'
e country, and shouting
abeth go home.'
Levesque, speaking beneath
quartered with the old
ch Valois fleur-de-lys,
inded his listeners that he
esented some 25% of
ada's twenty-five million
ulation, and said that
bec should reject the new
with Britain because it
ld weaken the province by
easing the powers of the
ominantly English-speaking
ral government. He spoke of
bec's destiny as a nation in
f, but emphasised that the
becois should try to realise
destiny within the political
ess and 'without hostility.'
ller, but significant rallies
held in four other Quebec
ns.
the majority, there was no
erestimating the feeling of
onal pride which
mpanied the staid, formal,

royal ceremony. 'Constitution
Finally Home' proclaimed the
Quebec Sunday Express in
letters an inch and a half high,
and 'Emotional Outburst Greets
Constitution's Homecoming,' in
a headline to an article speaking
of 'the dawning of a new era of
history.' It was without doubt an
historic occasion unprecedented
in living memory, and for most a
triumphant, if long delayed,
sequel to the story begun by the
four million Canadians who
became Dominion citizens in
1867.
The rain had stopped, but the
wind was just as mischievous as,
on 18th April, the Queen took
her leave of a Canada with a
newly-won status. Returning to
the airport where she had landed
three days earlier, she prepared
to board the same aircraft for her
flight back to London. Prince
Philip was with her but only to
the bottom of the aircraft steps.
He was on his way to America,
where he would be piloting the
new Rolls-Royce powered

Boeing 757 jetliner, recently
completed and tested in Seattle.
So there was a swift but
unprecedented public kiss (left)
as she went her way and, fifteen
minutes later, he went his.
Both were back home in time
for the Queen's 56th birthday
three days later, in the familiar
setting of Windsor Castle and in
the company of members of the
Royal Family. But the Prince and
Princess of Wales were
holidaying in the Scillies, and
Prince Andrew was heading for
the South Atlantic to prepare for
a confrontation in which,
ironically, Britain was seeking to
regain control of the tiny, long-
treasured possession of the
Falkland Islands, having just
ceded power, peacefully and
willingly, to the vast former
dominion of Canada.

The Badminton Horse Trials have their parallel in the Horse Show world in terms of permanence, excellence and royal patronage.

That well-established five day domestic equestrian event, the Royal Windsor Horse Show, took place from 12th to 16th May and as always the Royal Family was represented, though as at Badminton, in a purely private capacity. The Queen, who had missed Badminton because of the hastily-arranged visit to Ottawa to sign over the Canadian Constitution, did not

in spite of the looming conflict the South Atlantic, have to forego her usual attendance at Home Park Windsor.

The Show, which is held totally out of doors, brings together the varying skills of show-jumping, carriage driving, Pony Club games and dressage displays, as well as the spectacular military style entertainments by the King's Troop Royal Horse Artillery and the Household

Cavalry. This particular year the main interest in the show-jumping arena was drawn by the intense competition the British riders faced from several foreign entrants – the Australians, Belgians, Swedes and Libyans, all going for a total of £12,000 in prize money.

The Queen's presence on 14th, 15th and 16th May matched the days on which the International Carriage Driving Grand Prix, sponsored as usual by the London firm of estate agents, Messrs. Knight Frank & Rutley,

was held. This was no coincidence since, again as usual, the Duke of Edinburgh took part in that competition, in this, the tenth year of his career in competitive carriage driving in the international field.

The first day's competition centred around dressage, which covers a multitude of fine and well-scrutinised points of performance and style, such as the forward and backwards manoeuvring of the teams of horses while hitched to the carriages, the condition and presentation of both horses and carriages, and the dress, deportment and behaviour of the drivers themselves. Prince Philip (right and opposite page, top right) was as immaculate as ever with his black topper showing a perfect sheen, white cravat, brown leather gloves and regulation apron, his superbly turned-out metal-framed carriage and his equally well-groomed horses fresh from the Royal Mews.

Competition was keen, however, with George Bowman, seven times winner of the British National Championships,

heading no fewer than thirteen British competitors, and five further entrants from Europe and the United States. No wonder the Prince looked concerned, and the Queen thoughtful, as (left and opposite page far left) they watched and discussed the progress of the other riders. (With them, incidentally, was Prince Philip's youngest, and only surviving sister, Princess Sophie of

...er, now 72 and a regular
... to the Royal Windsor
... Show.)
...Queen, surrounded by
...ament officials and by
...ers of her staff, including
... right) the Crown
...ry, Lt-Col Sir John Miller,
...lf an accomplished four-in-

illustrious twenty-five year polo-
playing career. His choice of
what was then a relatively little-
known sport betrayed his typical,
almost perverse flair for trying
anything once, and he was
undeterred by its comparatively
novel and unrecognised status.
Indeed, the year before had seen

learn all there is to learn about
dealing with horses in any
context.
He probably realised this when,
after feeling understandably
pleased with himself at the end
of his first season, the following
one brought him down to earth
with a catalogue of disasters

large and small. The most
spectacular was the famous
accident at the Lowther Driving
Trials, the well-established
annual event at Shap, on the
edge of the Lake District, in
1972, when the rear of his
carriage hit a tree stump, and
horses, passengers – royal and

...l driver, was seen at her most
...ed, interested and animated
...e followed the fortunes of
...husband's many rivals round
...dressage course. Both Prince
...p and his team of horses
...ormed well, and their end-
...ay positions gave them a
...ue opportunity to carry off
...prize by the end of the
...nament.
...-in-hand carriage driving is
...Prince Philip's most
...uming competitive sport.
...ook it up in 1971, as he
...ismatically says, "because I
...ght it was the right thing to
...though his decision was
...e than probably prompted
...he mild arthritis in his hands
...ch effectively drew the
...ain on his enthusiastic and

only the first internationally
recognised carriage-driving
event, so the sport could hardly
be said to be very advanced in
respectability.
His apprenticeship, much of it
self-taught, lasted a couple of
hard-working years. He began
by mastering the art of guiding
single horses drawing carriages,
graduated to pairs of horses and
finally, with the aid of miniature
training courses which he
ordered to be laid out at
Windsor and Sandringham,
cracked the secret of coping with
four horses at a time. Perhaps
"cracking the secret" sounds too
final: it is in fact inaccurate, and
the Duke is nothing if not
disarmingly realistic, knowing
full well that you never quite

commoner – and conveyance were thrown all over the place. It was after that, when the righted carriage was found to be badly knocked about and not fit for further use without considerable expenditure on repairs, that he went in for metal-framed rather than wooden-framed vehicles. "I knew I was asking for all sorts of new trouble when I took it up," he once said, and his career from that point has proved his foresight. To the common herd, leaders and wheelers and swingletrees are so much equestrian jargon, and carriage driving is news only when carriages are upturned, wheels are stuck in mud, shoulders are dislocated, language turns blue, and drivers become thoroughly soaked in lakes and streams. In his time Prince Philip has been associated with all of these fond and, to those not directly involved, somewhat amusing visions, but he takes the knocks philosophically: "Anyone who is concerned about his dignity would be well advised to keep away from horses," he once wrote. "Horses are great levellers. I've got shoulders which would make interesting specimens for any medical school."

For all that, his 15 years in charge of the reins have

produced some satisfying resu[...] He has won prizes at competitions all over Great Britain, from Scotland to Cirencester, from Cheshire to Goodwood. In 1975, having come seventh in the Royal Scottish Championships, fifth Cirencester and a creditable fourth at Windsor, he was

...ed for the European ...g Championships in ...d, just two years after he ...mpeted internationally. In ...e captained the British ...in the World ...pionships and it came ...ictorious. In 1981 he was ...t the Windsor Horse Trials, ...h unplaced in the

enjoy in London.

The Queen has about three dozen ceremonial horses at the Royal Mews at any one time. The dozen or so greys are known as Windsor Greys (simply because their predecessors were kept at the Windsor stables until they were closed down just before the

importance until recently, is beginning to take over.

Prince Philip prefers the slightly nippier characteristics of part-bred Cleveland Bays and it was these he used at the Royal Windsor Horse Show in 1982. They stood him in good stead in the cross-country event, or Marathon, on 15th May, when

his own supple and authoritative horsemanship and the fitness of his team brought him through a near faultless round – even though his passengers may on occasion have experienced that frisson of fear which turns the knuckles white (below left). But the Queen looked pleased

...pean Championships in ...zerland. In all he has come ...nd four times at Windsor. ...vas hoping to improve on ...in 1982.

...h of his success must of ...se depend on his horses and ...as the good fortune to be ...to pick from the Royal ...s stock for each occasion. ...is not so outrageous as it ...t at first glance seem, since

the purpose to which the Queen's pageant horses are put is by and large that of pulling carriages. Granted, the events for which they are officially used are ceremonial, but this does not make them unsuitable for competitive carriage driving, and the occasional testing on a gruelling Horse Show course provides them with better exercise than they can ever

Second World War), or as Oldenburg Greys. The latter strain now predominates, and indeed were used to haul the Prince and Princess of Wales' 1902 State Postillion carriage from St Paul's Cathedral on their Wedding Day. Then there are two dozen bay horses, well represented by Oldenburgs, though the Cleveland strain, which has enjoyed secondary

enough with his performance (opposite page), while his youngest son Prince Edward (top), on weekend leave from Gordonstoun, was quietly impressed. It was hard to believe that his father was on the verge of his sixty-first birthday.

Next day, the obstacle course brought the competition to its end. The Queen, rather more formally dressed in a light suit –

a concession to the fact that she would later take part in the official formalities and prize-giving, sat in the stands with her sister-in-law (below and opposite page) recording the thrills and spills of the event with her ever-present camera. Prince Philip, back in formal dress again after the cloth cap and short sleeves of the day before, turned in another good performance and a clear round, and to his great delight, carried off first prize for the first time. His reward was a rosette from the Queen, to whom he respectfully doffed his topper (left) and a place in the

British team for the World Championships in the Netherlands in August. Prince Philip has rarely missed an opportunity to write or contribute to books on subjec close to his heart. He has in hi time written articles or forewo on yachting, painting, birds, th environment, flora and fauna and architecture. In 1983 his book on competitive carriage driving was published. His victory, one of many, at Royal Windsor – "the most satisfying win of my driving career" – should give the book all the authority it needs. Any buddin four-in-hand enthusiast should consider taking a leaf or two o of it.

Queen Mother, but the previous month it was announced that she would not be available, and the engagement was hastily tacked on to the Princess of Wales' schedule. As it happened it was an apt enough alternative. The Princess had early in February assumed the presidency of five organisations, four of them orientated towards benefiting young people, and one of them was the Albany Trust.

The Albany Trust is one of those little-known, very localised charities which achieve any degree of celebrity only on an occasion such as this. In fact it has long been associated with

Prompted in no small measure by a spell of warm weather, a colourful carnival atmosphere permeated the South East London suburb of Deptford when on 18th May the Princess of Wales performed the last of her official engagements before the birth of Prince William. She was there to open a new community centre, erected at a cost of almost £3 million through the good offices of the Albany Trust. The opening was to have been performed by the

the Royal Family – indeed it began under the auspices of none other than H.R.H. the Duchess of Albany. She was the wife of Queen Victoria's youngest, and only haemophiliac, son Prince Leopold (1853-1884), who in

1881 was created Duke of Albany. A homely, good-natured woman, she devoted her life to good causes, particularly after the death of her husband, to whom she had been married for less than three years.

One cause she espoused with

Eventually the exploitation was halted, but the Duchess and the Minister found that they had, well-meaningly but unwittingly, created their own little unemployment problem. With the prospect of seeing the girls on the streets making their own dubious efforts to employ themselves gainfully, the Duchess decided to put right the mischief she had created, and in 1894 established a Trust, which has borne her name ever since, designed to cater for the girls in their long hours of enforced idleness.

When the Duchess, whose sister Queen Emma was the great-

grandmother of the present Queen Beatrix of the Netherlands, died in 1922, her only daughter, the late Princess Alice, Countess of Athlone, took over the presidency, which she held until her own death fifty-nine years later at the age of 97. That was in January 1981. Two years earlier she had button-holed her great-great-nephew Prince Charles and persuaded him to lay the foundation stone of the Community Centre which his wife was now in Deptford to open formally (these pages).

The Princess of Wales spent over an hour at the centre, receiving the usual heaps of posies from the crowds she

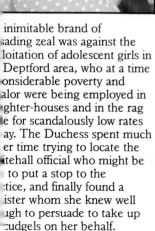

inimitable brand of
sading zeal was against the
loitation of adolescent girls in
Deptford area, who at a time
onsiderable poverty and
alor were being employed in
ghter-houses and in the rag
le for scandalously low rates
ay. The Duchess spent much
er time trying to locate the
itehall official who might be
to put a stop to the
tice, and finally found a
ister whom she knew well
ugh to persuade to take up
cudgels on her behalf.

spoke to during the visit, and looking at her most contented. She did not, however, forgo any opportunity to sit down nor, as one might have come by now to expect, to talk about babies. With her own confinement

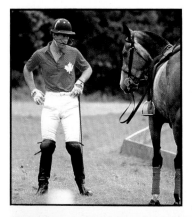

expected only six weeks later, the creche was the focus of great interest. She also met those who give their time voluntarily to help in the centre, watched a group of pensioners at a bingo session and visited the centre's restaurant – and it was here that mothers and children heard of the latest preparations for the royal birth.

The stories didn't quite tally and no-one was quite sure whether the Princess said that her baby *would* be a boy or that she hoped it would. "We'll just have to wait and see," she finally told 14-year-old David Rowland. She took one look at Mrs Patricia Woodgates' five-month-old twins and confessed "I don't think I could cope with a brace. I only hope I can cope with one

when the time comes." Mrs Woodgates warned her that "you don't learn much about them until you've actually had them," a remark that put into perspective the Princess' revelation to Mrs Doreen Markland, that Prince Charles had been studying books about pregnancy and baby care so feverishly of late that he had become "something of an expert. He keeps telling me what to do," she added, "and I don't like it!"

The visit came to an end with

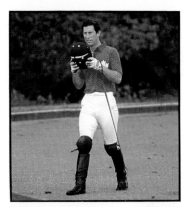

the presentation to the Princess of a picture of the community centre drawn by Mr Reg Rowlands, the Chairman of the New Cross Building Society. The old Duchess of Albany would have been proud of her achievement.

With official engagements over until October (as it was then thought) the Princess was expected to remain out of public sight for the foreseeable future. The precedent which had always

(these pages) in which he played for the Canadian side run by the biscuit heir Mr Galen Weston. It wasn't, however, the best of days: the wind was chilly and she ventured only short distances from the car, where she frequently sheltered, looking just a little bored.

kept royal ladies discreetly indoors during the visible stages of their pregnancies had already been broken and many people expected that time would now be called. But the Princess of Wales has not been called innovatory for nothing and she turned up in public almost as often as there was a polo match to see in which Prince Charles was playing. Giving the lie to the widely believed story, created out of her reactions to some pretty terrifying scenes on the field in 1981, that she disliked polo, she followed Prince Charles almost everywhere, pacing the perimeters with the informality for which she has become well known.

Thus on 22nd May she travelled with the Prince to Windsor Great Park for a weekend game

They change the Guard here, ambassadors are officially accredited here, an obscure Epiphany service is held in its chapel once a year, and in the old days Royal Levées were held here in what was then called "the Season."

One could be readily forgiven for supposing that, as far as official or public appearances are concerned, the Royal Family seems to take a dim view of St James's, and give it a wide berth.

St James's Palace is one of the more obscure of London's royal buildings. Not physically, for its long, Georgian-windowed walls can be skirted at any time of day by anyone wishing to get from Trafalgar Square to Piccadilly by road. But for all the security surrounding it, Buckingham Palace is known far more intimately than St James's. As the diplomatic focal point of the royal connection, St James's wears a reputation even more forbidding than its dark frontage.

Visits by its members are conspicuous by their rarity. The occasional concert, exhibition or fashion show is staged here from time to time, and may draw a royal audience or patron. This was where the Prince and Princess of Wales exhibited their wedding presents during two hectic and profitable months in 1981, and where Prince and Princess Michael of Kent have had their two children christened. Like every State Visitor to this country before

and since, the visiting Sultan of Oman came here to receive addresses of welcome in March 1982.

Both the Duke of Kent and his sister Princess Alexandra have their London offices here, and for the Kents, York House at the western end of the Palace is the official London residence.

So the Duchess of Kent did not have very far to come when on the morning of 24th May she made a very special presentation to fifty handicapped children.

Yard was spectacularly exciting. Each coach was festooned with balloons and streamers and would shortly take them all on a tour of London before their journeys back to their home towns.

The Duchess found the occasion both moving and enjoyable. With her well-earned reputation for being very much at home with children, she was irresistably drawn to these youngsters whose happiness

The Variety Club of Great Britain, which justly boasts of being the greatest children's charity in the world, had recently completed a massive fund-raising exercise to provide its famous Sunshine Coaches for the children of three schools in Bradford, Bristol and Seaford, Sussex. For handicapped children, outdoor activities are a vital part of the school curriculum and their first sight of their new means of indispensible transport arriving into Stable

depends so heavily on the goodwill of others. As she waved the last of the coaches off (above), their passengers carried with them special memories of their very royal day.

It all made for one of the happier and lighter sides of the otherwise very solemn, dignified and diplomatic character which traditionally surrounds the Court of St James's.

A five-week season of Tchaikovsky's "Swan Lake," performed at the London Coliseum by the London Festival Ballet, came to a royal climax on 25th May when the Ballet's Patron, Princess Margaret, attended a gala performance in aid of its Development Fund. This new production by John Field was certain to attract the Princess' attention: she has maintained a lifelong interest in the ballet – she became the first President of the newly formed Royal Ballet in 1957 as part of her more general musical appreciation. Music and its interpretation in the wider arts have been important to her,

continued to be well aired in public, with less private matters again distinguished by varying degrees of controversy.

The publication in October of Nigel Dempster's biography "HRH The Princess Margaret: A Life Unfulfilled" contained a detailed résumé of material the author had previously disclosed in his *Daily Mail* gossip column, and more. It was said to have been read in draft and approved by the Princess, but her former husband, Lord Snowdon, dismissed it as having been "written without interviews." Jocelyn Stevens, a friend of the Princess, weighed in, detailing its many inaccuracies in an

as she disclosed in the BBC programme "Desert Island Discs" in 1981, when she selected favourite recordings of ballet music as well as jazz and opera.

The Princess had undertaken, in the previous 12 months, her usual quota of public engagements – including visits abroad to attend the Diamond Jubilee of King Sobhuza II of Swaziland in September, to confer independence in Antigua in November, and to open an art exhibition at Houston, Texas in February. But she will, if she cares to, remember it as a time when issues in her private life

article in the *Daily Express* – a paper which itself ran a week-long serialisation about her, in competition with the book's serialisation in the *Daily Mail.* The statement in the book that she "would like to marry again" seemed to be confirmed by the many sightings of her with the 55-year-old widower Norman Lonsdale. They were photo-graphed together at a masked ball in November; he stayed with her on Mustique in February; and when the Princess was spotted wearing an unfamiliar ring on her engagement finger during an official visit to Glasgow in April, the rumour-mongers drew their

barred for the third time in four unhappy years from attending the Christmas Ball at Keele University of which she was Chancellor: nothing personal here; it was just that the left wingers in the Students' Union took objection to the police prowling around before and during royal visits. And she received her annual insult from Willie Hamilton MP who called her "a useless, middle-aged floozie" in front of 200 nurses and hospital workers as part of their campaign for higher pay. Sometimes she must wonder whether it's all worth it. Who'd be a Princess?

clusions. They were almost actively encouraged by tantalisingly ambiguous statements by both Mr Lonsdale and the Princess' private secretary, but when two days later HRH turned up at an NSPCC lunch with *three* rings on her engagement finger, and reserved denials were issued all round, the story magically vanished.

For good measure, the Princess was criticised quite severely for refusing – apparently on the grounds that it would spoil her hair-do – to wear a sterile bonnet at a medical products factory in Plymouth. She was

On 27th May, a welcome splash of colour on a drab day was provided by the comings and goings at Westminster Abbey where the Queen installed the latest crop of Knights Grand

is cocooned in time and place. In time, it is a comparatively short ritual surrounded by a grandiose religious service full of trumpetings, psalms of praise, patriotic music and the constant shifting of beadles, almsmen, genealogists and Scarlet Rod. In place, it happens in the inner sanctum of the Order's own chapel, the King Henry VII Chapel, away from the eyes of established Knights in the body of the Abbey.

Like most occasions of high ceremony, precision is of the essence. Gentlemen at Arms and Yeomen of the Guard officially took up positions at 10.57 am; Princess Alice arrived (bottom, far right and opposite page bottom left) with her lady in waiting Miss Jane Egerton-Warburton at 11.05; Prince Charles – Grand Master since

Cross of the Order of the Bath. As Sovereign of the Order she presided at this irregularly-staged embodiment of a tradition formalised in 1725. For, unlike the Garter Service, this is not an annual event: this year's ceremony was held to install those Knights appointed since 1978. There were eleven of them – five generals, four air marshals, an admiral and Lord Adeane, the Queen's former private secretary. Fortunately for all of them the bathing rite, from which the Order takes its title, has long since been dropped, though George I included it in the schedule of obligatory ceremonies on creating the Order out of the old medieval "Degree of Knighthood." The installation ceremony itself

who, as Grand Master, delivers it to the Senior of the Knights to be installed, so that they can all take the oath. This includes an undertaking to "defend maidens, widows and orphans in their rights and . . . suffer no extortion."

The Grand Master has then to seat the new Knights in their

stalls, but no sooner is this done than they have to rise again to go and stand beneath their respective banners.

Another pattern of synchronised movement precedes the Queen's obeisance before the altar as she offers gold and silver, as does the senior of the new Knights. There follows a ritual drawing and sheathing of swords, and exhortations to defend the Gospel and maintain the "Sovereign's Right and Honour," before the select gathering returns to rejoin the congregation.

A general thanksgiving and prayers are followed by the Blessing and the National Anthem, and the procession out through the East Cloister begins (left and far left). And a few words from the Queen and Prince Charles (opposite page) to a cluster of school-children convinces them that these robed and tiara'd figures with their magical symbols are pleasantly human after all.

75 – arrived (left) at 11.09;
d the Queen (far right) at
2.

e service takes much the
ne form as any Morning
vice, with psalm, lesson,
sicles and responses, prayers
anthems. Then a thin
cession of royalty and
ghts moves up the Abbey
t the High Altar and into the
g Henry VII Chapel, while
ems are sung. Once inside
Chapel the members of the
cession take their appointed
es – the Queen and Prince
rles have special stalls – and
except for the Knights about
e installed, who remain
ding. Bath King of Arms
ives a Book of Statutes from
Deputy Secretary and
eeds towards Prince Charles

There is nothing particularly new about the Queen of the United Kingdom meeting the Holy Father. Elizabeth II has met a succession of Popes – as Princess Elizabeth she was received by Pope Pius XII, and as Queen she called on Pope John XXIII in 1961, and on the present Pope in 1980 during each of her State Visits to Italy. Since Henry VIII broke with the Church of Rome, however, no

Protestants it had been stated that the meeting was not between Heads of Churches but between Heads of State. When the Falklands crisis became an issue the Argentinians were told that the meeting had no political, but only a religious, significance.

The Pope mollified the Argentinians by promising to visit them in June, and his tour of Britain and meeting with the Queen passed off quietly and satisfactorily. The Pope was met at the Palace by an official (far left) but the Queen came out to the Grand Entrance to bid him farewell personally.

Pope has ever set foot inside the United Kingdom, far less parleyed with the Sovereign. For that reason His Holiness' forty minutes with Her Majesty at Buckingham Palace on 28th May 1982 was one of the most historically significant events of her reign. As a meeting between Heads of State it was all a matter of ordinary diplomatic courtesy, but as a symbol of the coming together of two churches, whose rupture over four hundred years ago still excites powerful controversy, it had a potency all its own.

That was particularly so in the light of further controversy stirred up by news of his impending visit: the Orange Order branded the Queen as a potential "traitor to the Constitution" and Mr Enoch Powell said it was "constitutionally and logically impossible for England to contain both the Queen and the Pope." Then further difficulties arose with the Falklands crisis, the Argentinians claiming that the visit would bestow the unfair advantage of Papal blessing upon the British cause.

This led to a further confusion. Originally, to appease the ultra-

"Buckingham Palace – June 2: The Queen accompanied by the Duke of Edinburgh, Queen Elizabeth the Queen Mother, Princess Anne Mrs Mark Phillips, The Duke and Duchess of Gloucester, Prince and Princess Michael of Kent and Princess Alexander (sic) the Hon Mrs Angus Ogilvy and the Hon Mr Angus Ogilvy, honoured Epsom Races with her presence today."

It's a bit of a mouthful, even for the Court Circular, but as usual it relates only the bare facts of attendance or presence, and in this case without the additional details of how they all got there, what they did when they arrived, or how they travelled back. But

breed and race a Derby winner still continues, has rarely missed this most prestigious of the world's classic races and the most financially rewarding of the British classics. And it is a rare occasion when the majority of the Royal family do not accompany her.

more conservatively, wore her complete outfit of matching hat, coat and dress. Princess Anne was in a fresh, green dress, while the Duchess of Gloucester preferred bright white. Princess Michael at Epsom was indistinguishable from Princess Michael at Royal Ascot, with her stately

of arms or crowns affixed to their roofs. It was sudden and violent, as if to remind everyone who had come to enjoy this annual beano that the Falklands were closer than they might have thought. It sent some 300,000 people scurrying for shelter – girls in bikinis or ra-ras looked

then everyone knows that the Royal Family habitually have a ripping time at Epsom – it's almost as imperative as solemnity at the Opening of Parliament or hats at Ascot. The Queen, whose quest to

This year the Queen arrived coatless – unusually for her but the weather in the first week of June had for once turned up trumps and the sun beat down relentlessly for most of the afternoon. The Queen Mother,

ensemble and grand feathered hat.

A thunderstorm broke just after the impressive royal arrival – a procession of Rolls Royces purring up the course with badges displaying personal coats

never so out of place beneath picnic rugs and newspapers, a grown men, stripped to the wa and covered in sun tan oil, cowered under the nearest umbrellas.

An hour before the big race it

topped and the sun rejuvenated he festival atmosphere. Eventually the Royal party came down from the stand and inspected the 1982 Derby runners from the side of the course (bottom picture, the Queen Mother and the Queen with – left to right – Mr Ogilvy, Princess Alexandra, Prince Philip and – at the back in the centre – the Duke of Gloucester). As the expressions in the royal faces made clear, all were fascinated by the procession of these finely groomed horses cantering by at the peak of their fitness and form. They returned to the Royal Box where their every

The Queen had a cup of tea there and made a close inspection of the contents of the flower box. The 1982 Derby was as exciting, both in anticipation and on the day itself, as almost any of the two hundred-odd meetings of past years. The prize to the eventual winner was higher than ever, and the value in international stud fees would be phenomenal. Yet, for once, there were no royal histrionics or the customary excited gesticulations as the runners came home. The Queen's personal interest seemed more dispassionate than in previous years. Perhaps that was because, in the hour of war, Peacetime only came seventh.

gesture could be watched: Princess Anne discussed with her father (opposite page, left), the Queen with her mother (opposite page, right) and Princess Michael with everyone (above and centre pictures).

Or perhaps because, as Susan Sangster's horse Golden Fleece ran in the winner, the Queen knew she had yet another year to wait before her chance came up again.

This was one of the last public appearances the Princess of Wales made before the birth of her baby and she might justifiably have looked back on it all with a degree of satisfaction. It had been a public, almost as

soon as it had been a private fact, that she was with child, and the very public interest must have made it an extremely long pregnancy indeed.

Though it began in a glow of public congratulation – the Lord Mayor of London likened the news to a hallmark on the gold ingot of the Royal Wedding, and the Prince of Wales praised "the wonderful effect my dear wife has had on everyone" – excesses of publicity threatened at times to turn the whole thing sour and cause the mother-to-be to modify her flexible, informal approach to her royal duties. Over-zealous photographers plagued her at Highgrove and Tetbury and again on the

Bahamian holiday, and were rebuked by the Queen for doing so. Even the BBC was considered to have gone too far with a comedy sketch showing the Princess giving evidence in a court case against a contraceptive firm. Rumours abounded that American and British firms were in the process of making feature films about her courtship with the Prince of Wales, one of them containing "details not revealed before," but the finished products were bland and disappointing. Artists had a field day. Bryan Organ's official painting of the Princess was slashed at the National Portrait Gallery, where it now hangs restored and protected by Perspex. The wedding was celebrated on canvas by Sue Ryder, who portrayed the Princess in a froth of light, filmy bridal silk, but avoiding over-sentimentality. Ruskin Spear painted the Prince

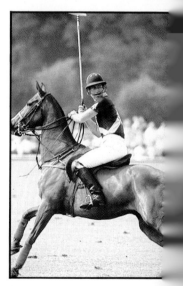

and Princess kissing on Buckingham Palace balcony, but over-emphasised what was in reality a fleeting peck almost into a clinch. Carol Payne went one worse and exhibited a painting at Plymouth showing

the royal couple in more intimate surroundings.

The speculation about twins must have sickened her at times. The baby's sex was universally discussed and the general plumping for a boy proved

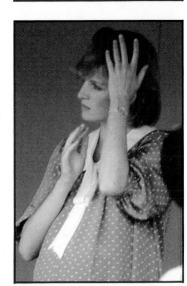

inspired. The place of its birth divided the country – Highgrove, Buckingham Palace and St Mary's Paddington were all candidates. The suppliers of baby clothes, maternity wear, nursery furniture, equipment and toys, became the target of endless Press detective work. (Incidentally, the doll trade was

thrilled: "This is definitely the year of the baby doll," said one manufacturer.) Even the Princess' own bedroom, with the chance of housing a four-poster bed more than once slept in by the French courtesan, Diane de Poitiers, excited interest.

If ever the Princess had properly acquired an image, it changed over this period. She seemed less vulnerable than before her marriage and rumours that she was decisive, unyielding, even precociously ambitious began to spread. Certainly photographers caught her more than once letting everyone know of some displeasure. In five months she was held responsible for having sacked Prince Charles' valet and two of her own detectives and

she was widely reported to have taken on the Queen over whether her baby should accompany her on future royal tours abroad. And she appears to have chosen the baby's nanny herself.

If one thing is totally beyond doubt it is that the codes of public behaviour as they affect

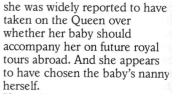

princes and princesses of the Blood Royal and their spouses have changed fundamentally and irrevocably. From the relative obscurity of a position as the youngest daughter of an Earl, the Princess has become the wife of the heir to the Throne, but she has brought to the monarchy as an institution all the best elements of uninhibited social and personal behaviour. It raised eyebrows at first, this free and easy chat with the common herd, this touching of other people's babies, those giggling larks with young children. But no chord with the public was more sympathetically struck, and no more timely boost to the

monarchy's popularity was ever so comprehensively furnished or maintained. And all, it seems, without effort.

That statement may imply that it is easy to "become" a member of the Royal Family and to assimilate its ways, its taboos, its "image." That may or may not be the case – only the Princess herself and her mentor Lady Susan Hussey can verify, and for obvious reasons they are not available for comment. It probably comes nearer the truth to say that the Princess has modified what everybody thought was the fixed, unchanging manner of royalty whenever it appeared in public. If so she is accomplishing this not through perversity or even as the result of a conscious decision. She has clearly accepted Prince Charles' hand in marriage and the monarchy's soul for life on terms which reflect her own uncomplicated values as much as the institution's complexities and quaintness. The public have been easily won over, and the Royal Family is demonstrably not far behind.

Five years ago to the day, Britain was in the grip of the Queen's Silver Jubilee celebrations. On 7th June 1982 the country watched the unfolding of one of those perennial chapters of the Queen's reign which have given it its distinctive character. It was another in a long line of "firsts," for just over a week after Pope John Paul II had been the first Pontiff to meet the Sovereign on British soil, Ronald Reagan, the fortieth President of the United States of America, became the first to be welcomed as a guest of the Queen at Windsor. It was an interesting triangular coincidence that the President and the Pope had met in Rome immediately before the visit to Windsor.

Due to arrive at Heathrow Airport at six o'clock in the evening, the President was almost half an hour late, owing to an industrial dispute at Rome Airport. But Prince Philip, looking somewhat incongruous in morning suit, waited, casting his eyes skyward for signs of the aircraft or looking around him at the charmless views of the cargo terminal on one side and the quarantine quarters on the other.

A blue and white Boeing 707, officially named "Presidential Air Force One," flew into sight and an army of police marksmen on top of buildings and ringing the tarmac, settled into position. Twelve of Britain's crack marksmen and a large contingent of the President's 150 bodyguards were amongst them.

The landing was good, and the President, in dark blue suit and red tie, emerged hearty and smiling to a warm, genial greeting from the Queen's husband (pictures below). Mrs Reagan, on her second trip to Britain – the first was for the Royal Wedding – looked thrilled to be here again.

The Prince and his guests spent a few minutes chatting together before the President, waving and giving the thumbs-up to admirers on top of the airport building, was brought to the line of ministerial celebrities, led by the Prime Minister. After five minutes of formal presentations, Prince Philip led the President and his lady back to where a couple of American Marine Corps Sea King helicopters were waiting. They boarded one of them, and accompanied by the reserve machine and by two dull-green escort helicopter gunships, choppered off for Windsor.

The Queen had received the signal that her guests were on their way and, wearing a bright yellow outfit, was ready and waiting on the lawns just outside the private apartments of the

e. With her, formally
ed, like his father, was the
e of Wales. The
dential helicopter landed
r and its three august
pants stepped out (below
e) and marched across the
(right and far right) for
istoric meeting with the
n and her heir (below).
e was a short bow from Mr
an, but no curtsey from his
for the Queen. Mrs Reagan

too often been on the
ving end of criticism back
e for bending the knee to
lty and had decided to
at the attitude she had
oted for her visit in 1981 – a
ial handshake but not a
e deferential gesture.
conversations were brief:
e were official ceremonies to
ot through. The party
ed up the steps to the
en garden against the East
ace of the Castle, and
ugh the Chester Tower to

the Quadrangle – very much the
inner sanctum of the Queen's
private residence. At 200 yards
long and eighty wide it is big
enough to accommodate a
sizeable reception committee,
and it was there in the form of
the 1st Battalion Grenadier
Guards.
The Queen led the President,
while Prince Philip, Mrs Reagan
and Prince Charles followed, to
the East Wall of the Quadrangle
where a carpet marked the
saluting base, and their arrival

was greeted with the rousing strains of the British and American national anthems (top right). As it happened, Mrs Reagan was out of line: protocol demanded that the Queen and the President should stand level with each other, but that their respective spouses should be a pace or two back. Prince Philip, who should know the ropes by now, complied as if it all came naturally, but Mrs Reagan stepped forward at the last moment, hand reverently on her heart as the band played. The Queen tried unsuccessfully to put things right without being obtrusive but gave up as Prince Philip resignedly shrugged his shoulders.

gave a private dinner for her guests in the State dining room. Having met the Queen Mother, the Princess of Wales, Princess Anne and Captain Mark Phillips, they sat down to a meal of fillet of haddock, breasts of chicken stuffed with mangoes, and raspberry jam-filled

Prince Philip then escorted Mr Reagan over to the lines of Guardsmen for the Presidential inspection of the guard of honour (right and top centre), and a march-past (below centre) followed their return to where the Queen and Prince Charles were waiting with Mrs Reagan. Prince Philip returned to provide her with some company as the parade passed them (right and below right). Then, the formalities over, the entire party moved off towards the private apartments. Again, protocol was the victim. Instead of walking with the Queen, the President motioned his wife to go first – "It's an old Reagan family custom," said his Press Secretary afterwards. But by then nobody seemed to mind these understandable lapses and the short journey through the Sovereign's Entrance past the splendidly-dressed Military Knights, proceeded on its way. Shortly afterwards the Queen

pancakes with whipped cream. All with the necessary liquid refreshment – white wine, a Chateau Batailley claret, champagne and vintage port. The President left the Castle that evening to attend a reception at the American Embassy in London and was greeted by a noisy demonstration from 2,000 people, including fifty MPs, protesting against America's "nuclear madness" and her support of some right-wing South American regimes. "He is not," said the demonstration's leader, "welcome in this country." An earlier demonstration by eighty women,

who blockaded the Stock Exchange in protest against cruise missiles in Britain, resulted in eleven arrests. It all contrasted strangely with the Royal Horse Artillery's gun salute in Hyde Park as the President had stepped from his aircraft onto British soil that evening.

The President and his wife slept that night in the Lancaster Tower of the Castle, overlooking the famous Long Walk into Home Park. Their suite included two bedrooms, hung with portraits of long-dead royal ancestors, two bathrooms, a dressing room dotted with miniatures and a drawing room containing salmon-pink sofas and chairs, and draped with Victorian-embroidered cream curtains. A gallery of Stubbses and Canelettos encrusted the connecting corridors.

By seven the next morning the visitors were awake: perhaps earlier if the sound of aircraft

approaching Heathrow Airport had disturbed them. "We're used to it," the President told the Queen. "Our home is right by the National Airport in Washington. We have the same problem." Be that as it may, there was a light breakfast of bacon and eggs before they were whisked off to the Royal Mews, where a special royal ride was to begin.

A dispassionate observer of the arrangements negotiated between the Royal Household and the White House in respect of this hour-long diversion might be forgiven for imagining that it was one of the greatest and most significant sixty minutes of the present millennium, and certainly bigger and better than anything seen either in Mr Reagan's days in Hollywood or on the battlefield at Dettingen where King George II became the last British monarch to lead

natural light to dispense with the need for floodlighting. And ultimately the army of bodyguards and security advisers was whittled down to a mere platoon.

In this spirit of Anglo-American compromise, the Queen's long-maintained love for life in the saddle, and the President's equally long experience of it on the film sets of Hollywood, came together that morning in a gentle, hour-long ride through Windsor's glistening parkland. The Queen had chosen her 8-year-old horse Centennial – a gift from the Canadian Mounties – for the President, since he was "a nice, obedient horse" with a reputation for being staid and eminently manageable. In fact the President found him a little frisky and struggled at times to keep him on a short rein. The Queen, riding her 20-year-old mare Burmese (left), had no such trouble. The horse had come through 1981's great

his army into battle.

For a Presidential delegation had visited Windsor earlier in the year to finalise security arrangements and had, it is reported, attempted to turn the entire episode into a pictorial extravaganza. They detailed the way they would like the Queen to ride, hoped that the shrubbery in the Long Walk could be suitably floodlit, and insisted on an accompanying posse of security men. In nearly all respects their requests were not met, the Queen feeling that the normal arrangements for photographers and film crews would, subject to some minor concessions, be sufficient and that there would be enough

Trooping drama with flying colours: this was a piece of cake Neither the Queen nor the President wore helmets, and so provoked adverse comment, implied or expressed, from the Pony Club, the Jockey Club an the Royal Society for the Prevention of Accidents. The Queen herself would have had some comment, it seemed, on the President's banter with Pressmen who bellowed questions at him which he felt compelled to answer as the Queen waited impatiently for him to get on with the ride. Behind them, separated only b a Range Rover full of detective came Prince Philip, indulging a spot of four-in-hand driving

cause in the Falklands by congratulating him on "putting freedom on the offensive, where it ought to be." The President responded by calling her "foreseeing and courageous, returning her country's people to the roots of their strength with the eloquence and determi-

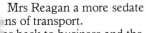

Mrs Reagan a more sedate ...ns of transport.
...as back to business and the ...ident returned to the Castle ...repare for a working lunch at ...0 Downing Street, where he

was met by Mrs Thatcher in a ceremony at the front door (above). In her speech of welcome she made a point of implying her appreciation of his ultimate support for Britain's

nation necessary to lead."
The same sentiments emerged
at a scintillating State banquet
held in St George's Hall at
Windsor Castle that night,
(these pages) at which the entire
adult complement of the Royal
Family were present – except the
Princess of Wales and the Queen
Mother, who was away on her
annual tour of the Channel
Ports. The royal ladies glittered
in their magnificent assortment
of tiaras, and the gentlemen
glowed in their Windsor uniform
with the bright red collars and
cuffs ordained by King George
III.
After dinner – Balmoral salmon,
lamb in Madeira sauce with
spinach, cauliflower and
croquette potatoes, followed by
strawberries and cream with
meringue – the Queen formally
welcomed the President in a
speech which confirmed the
mutual admiration in which the
two countries held each other:
"Our commitment to a common
cause has led us to fight in two
World Wars and to continue to

stand together in defence of
freedom."
Then with a bluntness which
could only have been prompted
by a Prime Minister knowing
her country was on the verge of
victory in the South Atlantic, the
Queen turned to the Falkland
Islands. "These past weeks," she
said, "have been testing ones for
this country, when once again we
have had to stand up for the
cause of freedom. The conflict
was thrust on us by naked
aggression and we are naturally
proud of the way our fighting
men are serving their country.
But throughout the crisis we
have drawn comfort from the
understanding shown by the
American people. We have
admired the honesty, patience
and skill with which you have
performed your dual role as ally
and intermediary. In return we
can offer an understanding of
how hard it is to bear the
daunting responsibilities of
world power."
The President in reply took the
opportunity to review his own

stand on questions involving
world power, and spoke on
Poland, the Soviet Union,
terrorism and the Middle East.
Significantly he implied his
continued support for Britain i
the Falklands: "Young men ar
fighting not for mere real estat
but for the belief that aggressio
must not pay. Together,
committed to the preservation
freedom and our way of life, w
must strengthen a weakening
international order."
His speech, which a dozen of
staff had sweated over for wee
previously, and to which the
President had himself added t
final flourishes less than forty-
eight hours before, distilled th
essence of his country's
justification for remaining aloo
from the politics of the Falkla
conflict – even-handed, they
called it at the time – until th
gloves were off. Britain was
critical then, but relations we
now at their friendliest as the
Queen presided over this
glittering formal reconciliatio

If truth be told it was not actually completed until 1692 but the 66 acres of land were bought in 1682 and work on the institution "for the relief of such Land Souldiers . . . lame or infirme in the Service of the Crowne" began the same year. Its full name, the Royal Hospital, derives from its founding by King Charles II, the "Merry Monarch," whose restoration in 1660 led the monarchist, and in events somewhat reactionary, backlash against the austerities of Puritan Britain.

The annual parade has for decades enjoyed royal patronage

Thursday 10th June 1982 was a day of anniversaries. Eight years before, the Duke of Gloucester, the last surviving child of King George V, died. It was also Prince Philip's sixty-first

birthday: guns boomed again in Hyde Park and at the Tower; flags fluttered brightly from public buildings. Which was nice because it was also the day on which the Queen, as a special mark of her affection for the Chelsea Pensioners, chose to celebrate with them the three hundredth anniversary of the founding of their Hospital.

and this special royal visit added calibre and a grand sense of occasion to the colourful vision of the lines of red-coated in-pensioners (above) and the Romanesque statue of "our Pious Founder," swathed in oak leaves (top left) as a reminder of his hiding place after the Battle of Worcester in 1651. Figure Court was alive with the shuffle

of scarlet, the winking of a thousand medals, the brisk pacings of commanding officer in black, and the gentler social movements of the Queen. Dressed in a soft mauve outfit that was to become a favourite this summer, she reviewed 43 men, the able-bodied during marchpast (above) and the others sitting on benches, bla

nes nodding and walking-
s wagging as they hoped for
hance of a word with the
en as she passed (right and
w right).

a sobering thought that at
ears of age, one of them
l claim to have served in
3oer War in the last dim
ner of the reign of her
-great-grandmother Queen
ria. Others took part in
aigns in India as far back as
. Over a hundred of the
ital's present complement
d in the First World War,
nearly 250 in the Second.
roll call of their foreign
ce recall Britain's inter-war

imperial interests – Palestine,
Iraq, East Africa and Aden.
Between them, the in-
pensioners share no fewer than
250 gallantry medals and awards
for outstanding service, from the
Order of the British Empire to
the Belgian Albert Medal.
King Charles II's foundation of
the Hospital grew out of his
recognition of the importance of
his army. He would be gratified
by the knowledge that after
three hundred years the
Hospital, and the royal
connection, were still thriving.

e were no new Knights of
Order of the Garter to be
ted in 1982, so the Throne
n of Windsor Castle was
ft of ceremony on 14th June.
here was a meeting of the
r, as usual, and a luncheon
ich all the Knights taking
in the afternoon's service
present, along with the
rs of the Order and the
s.
s ever permissible to talk of
Garter ceremony as low-key,
ear's proceedings fitted the
ription. Relatively speaking
urse. The ceremonial is in
ce as spectacular, the

colour as vivid, the applause as
warm as always, but there was
no doubt that some earlier
ceremonies had the edge.
The buzz of speculation centred
first and foremost on the
Princess of Wales: she was here
last year as Lady Diana Spencer
– would she attend again today
in her new capacity? Spectators
craned their necks and swore
they'd seen her, but in fact she
never appeared. No foreign
royalty either. Two years before
both the Queen of Denmark and
the Grand Duke of Luxemburg
had attended, to add their own
brand of informality on the

windswept steps of St George's
Chapel. Today it was as if King
Farouk's prophecy – "One day
there will be only five kings left
– of Britain, hearts, clubs,
diamonds and spades" – had
come true.
Even the Duke of Edinburgh
was absent: at short notice he
had left London Airport that
morning to attend the funeral of
King Khalid of Saudi Arabia – a
State Visitor to Britain in 1981 –
who had died the previous day,
and to pay his respects and
convey the Queen's condolences
to his brother and successor
Crown-Prince Faud.
Thus, for once, the Queen
walked alone in the procession
which formed inside the Castle
and snaked down the Grand
Staircase to the Grand Entrance
where the ten Military Knights
of Windsor, in scarlet tunics with
white sashes, and the thirteen
tabarded heralds and
pursuivants joined to form the
vanguard of the procession.
Between them and the
Sovereign came eighteen

Knights, incredibly resplendent in their heavy, rich, blue mantles and white plumes shifting restlessly in a stiffish, though by no means unpleasant breeze. Sir Harold Wilson – one of the few recognisable faces, or names for that matter – waved cheerily, even royally. He was the only one to do so, as if all the applause were being accorded exclusively to him. The Knights were followed by the Queen Mother, with the Prince of Wales as her escort, and the applause grew pointedly louder.

The Queen, her face almost framed by the sweeping lines of

Coronation much of its distinctive and memorable flavour. It lasted an hour and included an ethereal, florid motet setting of one of the Psalms – a Latin elegiac version of Psalm 150 by the sixteenth-century organist and composer William Byrd.

The procession back was more, and less, spectacular than the arrival. More, because the Royal Family used carriages to take them back up the hill to the Castle: the Queen was joined by the Prince of Wales, the Queen Mother by the Duke of Beaufort. Less, because the

her plumed cap, looked defiantly young and palpably happy in the leisurely walk towards St George's Chapel as, section by section, the thousands of spectators, ticket-holders and invitees, rose to applaud her as they had done her mother and son. Soldiers of the Life Guards and the Blues and Royals, distinguishable by their white and red plumes respectively, studded the route on either side.

The service was relayed to those outside through unseen loudspeakers, and was full of the sounds – like Walton's *Te Deum* and Gordon Jacob's National Anthem – which gave the

Rome, nor the demotion by the Vatican of the Order's patron saint, St George, nor the scepticism of a generation speeding on towards the twenty-first century, have diminished the pleasurable tradition of its virtually annual celebration. The week ushered in by the splendour of the Garter ceremony continued with splendour of another kind, difficult to regard as formal and official, but as inescapably British as any military parade. On the Tuesday following Garter Day and for the three remaining days of the week, the eyes of the horse-racing fraternity were turned to, and fixed on, Royal Ascot.

Not only the horse-racing fraternity of course. Royal Ascot is as synonymous with hats as with horses and the expectation of four days of seeing and being seen on Ascot's sweeping course-side lawns or in its

Knights, few of them in the flower of youth, took cars. And eventually the Guards arranged themselves back into units and marched off as well.

Edward III had, for most of his comparatively long life, a sense of proportion, and would have been more than surprised to know that the Order of the Garter which, according to legend, he founded after picking up a lady's garter and placing it, jokingly, upon his own leg, was still alive and flourishing in the dying years of the twentieth century. Neither the breach with

fashionable bars and restaurants is as likely to draw any socialite or sartorial expert as is the opportunity to be in the unsaddling enclosure when the Gold Cup winner comes in.

Any venture into the social scene in Britain leads to excess and the unavoidable juggernaut of commercial marketing makes it chic to run publicity stunts against the respectable and respected Ascot background. Thus the camera crews are always looking for Mrs Shilling in her outrageous creations, or spying on some advertising

Anne who directed the laying-out of the Ascot course almost three hundred years ago and the presence of her equally enthusiastic successor today symbolises the continuing, though not unbroken, equestrian sympathies for which the Royal Family is well-known.

The Queen's continued patronage of the event also embodies a social statement of precedence and authority within that now amorphous section of society which is content to look to her for an indefinable leadership, an annual stamp of approval and encouragement for

agency's furtive attempts to place models in the correct setting as they brandish glasses of wine, sport summer fashions or purse lips caked with the latest cosmetic preparation.

It is hard to see where the Royal Family might fit into this, but its members enter into the four-day festival with as much gusto, in their restrained royal way, as anyone. It was of course Queen

the respectable in a world where respectability enjoys a declining role.

The grand entrance and arrival say it all. A line of carriages bowls at casual pace through Ascot's famous Golden Gates and an unstoppable surge of people rushes towards the rails for a fleeting glimpse of the procession, thin and silent in an immensely wide expanse of turf, being hauled by. Similarly, a crowd of spectators in the Royal Enclosure makes way for the royal progress on foot to the Royal Box in the Queen Elizabeth II Stand, and the front

Queen Mother looking like – well, looking like the Queen Mother, in her favourite pale coats and chiffon dresses. Prince Philip missed out on Tuesday and Friday; Princess Margaret wore her azalea Royal Wedding outfit and made nonsense of the rumours that she is no friend of the éclatante Princess Michael (opposite page, centre), and it was so very easy to see why the Duchess of Kent has been described as one of the seven most sophisticated women in the world.

lines of ladies in competing hats compete also for the chance to catch the royal eye (opposite page, bottom right).

From 15th to 18th June the ritual was enacted again before crowds whose numbers promised to exceed the record. More hopes of seeing the Princess of Wales perhaps? If so they were disappointed. On no day did she join the carriage procession and only on one did she slip quietly into the Royal Box, having arrived unobtrusively by car. In fact there was no day when the Family was wholly represented. The Queen and Queen Mother attended on all four days, the Queen looking particularly chic in a beige-coloured scalloped coat and matching hat, and the

Like all other members of the Royal Family, the Queen and Prince Philip pay several visits to Scotland in the course of the year, in addition to the long summer holiday at Balmoral and their occasional Spring weekends there. It has long been a custom, however, for them to spirit was enormously helped by the installation of the railways, of which she made such comprehensive use that the steam engine might seem to have been invented specifically for her.

During this week, the Queen and her husband reside

acknowledge this part of the kingdom by a special week-long visit, with each day packed with engagements taking them to all parts of the lowlands. This practice has its origins in Queen Victoria's reign. Her personal love of Scotland prompted her to make frequent visits north of the Border, and her pioneering

anently at their official
ence in Scotland, the Palace
olyroodhouse, and the
n's personal bodyguard for
uration is the three
red-year-old Royal
pany of Archers.
and, which was the first
of the United Kingdom

Cathedral Edinburgh at which
two new Knights of the Order of
the Thistle were installed – Lord
Elgin and Lord Thompson. The
Service, which is an annual one,
took place in the Order's Chapel
which occupies a small
extension to the Cathedral, and
the ceremonial included the

formation of the Royal
Company of Archers as the
Queen's bodyguard, and music
from the band of the Gordon
Highlanders.
The visual impact of the Thistle
ceremony (this page) is similar
to that of the Garter, although
the surroundings – Parliament

Square in Edinburgh – are not
so imposing as Windsor Castle.
But the rich, flowing robes are
there, the handsome white
plumes are there, and the long
stately procession of Knights
follows a pattern similar to the
Windsor ceremony. Unlike
Windsor, however, the Thistle
service is held in the morning,
with the traditional luncheon
taking place at Holyroodhouse
afterwards.
The Order of the Thistle has its
roots in the 15th century, but
Queen Anne made the last of
several revivals in 1703.

ally to greet the Queen
g her Silver Jubilee tour of
always looks forward to
days each year when the
reign's attention is
ntrated solely on matters
of the Border. At no time
excitement and sense of
nal identity greater than
the royal couple attend the
s' Ball and the great
nonies of the Order of the
le.
32 the Pipers' Ball, or the
Scottish Pipers' Society
to give it its full name,
rated its centenary and the
nbly Rooms in royal
ourgh looked especially
e. The Queen and Prince
are seen (left) arriving, on
uly, accompanied by the
man of the Centenary
mittee, and (centre left)
Sir James Morrison-Low,
ociety's Honorary Pipe-
.
r that day the Queen and
of Edinburgh had
ded a service in St Giles'

William.
The Duchess' visit to Stoneleigh came two days before she and the Duke celebrated their tenth wedding anniversary. They still share the modest, retiring sort of nature which craves obscurity and the peace of the countryside, and which – by some accounts – prompted them to plan setting up home on the Isle of Dogs before Prince William's early and tragic death at the age of 30 left them with the prospect, which soon materialised, of public duty for life. In 1983, Princess Alice paid tribute to their dedication. "They work incomparably harder than we did before the war," she wrote. "But," she added, as an example of relative financial strictures, "for much of his day's business, the Duke dodges about London on a motorbike."

The Duchess of Gloucester was among the visitors to the Royal Show on 6th July, touring part of the massive site which for many years has found a permanent home at Stoneleigh in Warwickshire. No branch of the Royal Family is more readily associated with farming than the Gloucesters. The late Duke ran farms at the country home, Barnwell Manor in Northamptonshire, in partnership with his wife, Princess Alice, and their elder son Prince

(these pages) she was in the Home Counties, visiting Croham Hurst Place, a home for the Blind at Sanderstead in Surrey. This was one of her last public

s patron of the London ssociation of the Blind, rincess Alexandra attended its 25th Anniversary celebrations rly in July. On 27th July

duties before a two-month summer break. A new schedule of appointments beginning in October included a ten-day visit to Thailand as the guest of King Bhumibhol and Queen Sirikit, for the 200th anniversary celebrations of the Chakri

dynasty. Princess Alexandra's son James took a family photograph marking his parents' departure for Bangkok: a keen photographer, he used an automatic release so that he could be included in the picture along with his parents and sister Marina.

regatta. Taking the helm in the Yeoman class yacht which has served him for many years, and casting only an occasional, furtively suspicious eye at the photographers (below) he crosse the line in second place, only 90 seconds behind the winning craft, Highland Fling. After attending a Royal London Yacht Club reception and a Royal Yack Squadron Ball at Cowes Castle the following day, he boarded the Royal Yacht *Britannia* on 3rd August for Balmoral, and anoth Highland fling, before visiting Holland to compete in the Worl Driving Championships.

The Queen has occasionally been there, Prince Charles has often raced and windsurfed there, Princess Anne and Prince Edward used to sail there and Princess Alexandra and her husband Mr Angus Ogilvy were frequent spectators there. But Prince Philip is the one member of the Royal Family for whom attendance at part of Cowes Week at least is an annual event. He was there again on 1st August, competing for the Queen's Cup – the major award in the Royal Southampton Yacht Club's opening

to go the way of many of his other outdoor interests, it was a day when he wore two teams' shirts – one for the Maple Leaf team, and one for Les Diables Bleus – and had no inhibitions about changing them in public. Nor did he think twice about

The Princess of Wales, keeping a low profile save for one official appearance at the Falklands service in London a few days before, was absent from Cowdray Park in Sussex on 2nd August. For her husband, whose enthusiasm for polo has refused

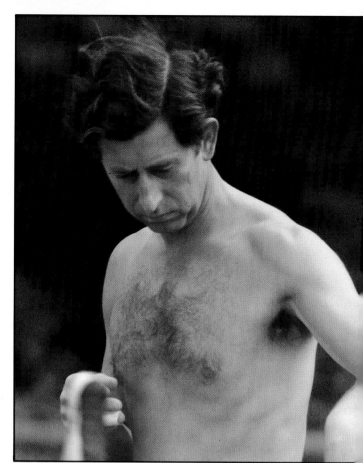

lodging behind the most convenient hedge to answer the inevitable call of nature as inconspicuously as possible (far right), nor again about nailing the old myth that royalty is not to be seen with glass in hand, let alone drinking from it (opposite page, top left). This was one of his last

adventures on the polo field. By the middle of August he and the Princess had made for Balmoral to join the Queen on her annual Highland holiday, leaving the English polo season to play out its last couple of weeks. Normally that would have meant no more polo for almost ten months, but in the event his tour of Australia in March 1983 gave him the opportunity to

limber up again for a couple of matches at Warwick Farm near Sydney. Understandably he found himself a little rusty after seven months off the field, but nevertheless contrived to be on the winning side on both occasions, justifying his commendable handicap of four with some well-praised shots, yet unable to avoid one of those legendary falls from the saddle.

It did not wholly comprise British royalty, because King Constantine of the Hellenes was in it, a representative of Greek royalty in exile and/or the Queen's vast and increasing cousinhood, royal or otherwise. With him was his wife, Queen Anne-Marie – the younger sister of the Queen of Denmark. In the King's team was his more immediate cousin the Duke of Kent (below left), the Duke's brother-in-law the Hon. Angus Ogilvy (opposite page, top right) and Captain Mark Phillips (opposite page centre), rejoicing in overall victory.

The Team's victory was not much

On 8th August, the North Wales Shooting School on Deeside was the scene of an assembly of no fewer than eight royalties. They took part in a celebrity challenge shooting match organised by the champion racing driver Jackie Stewart, between eight not-too-loosely formed groups of guns. Most competitors were from the worlds of sport and entertainment, but the competition was graced by the inclusion of two rather upmarket teams. One, headed by the Earl of Lichfield, represented Britain's aristocrats and was named The Lords. The other represented Britain's royalty and, avoiding any charge of vulgarity by calling themselves The Royals, opted for a much more classy put-down in the title The Team.

present and load new cartridges while the competitors held the guns open. In this way Princess Alexandra, her daughter Marina Ogilvy, Princess Anne and the Queen of Greece took an active and, as the stewards overruled objections by the runners-up, successful part in securing victory for royalty – a lesson, perhaps, in how to survive in a world of republics. Lord Lichfield (bottom left) was not amused.

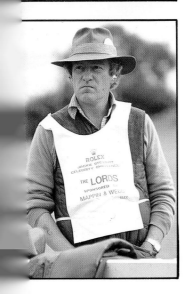

appreciated by the other contestants. The last and crucial round – in contrast to the more sedate standard clay-pigeon shoot or the picking off of dummy hares between straw bales – involved a marathon shoot of clay-pigeons propelled into the air at random. Time was of the essence and the reloading of guns had to be done quickly. Contestants in all other teams took up and put in their own cartridges but, shooting last, The Team engaged their respective ladies to

The increasing modern-day demand for the dramatic made it almost obligatory that, on her return journey from the Falklands conflict, *HMS Invincible* should not arrive home unless she loomed out of the fog in the process. Circumstances obliged on 17th September. Through the murk, almost six months after she had left amid a frenzy of patriotism and good wishes, *Invincible* slipped noiselessly towards her home harbour, her flight decks puddled with precipitation and patterned with Harrier jets and Sea King helicopters. Beside one of them stood the latest member of the British Royal Family to go to war, Sub-Lieutenant HRH Prince Andrew. Looking confident after his ordeal, feeling ineffably pleased and relaxed after a return journey taken up more with parties and sunbathing than with military exercises, he now awaited the culmination of his experience – to be reconciled with his family and to be part of one of the most patriotically effusive public welcomes any part of the British Isles had seen in almost forty years.

The Queen, now well over half way through her summer holiday at Balmoral, and Prince Philip, shortly to leave for Brisbane to open the Commonwealth Games, arrived with Princess Anne at Portsmouth Dockyard and were taken by barge to Spithead, two miles out to sea. From the bobbing barge they climbed up narrow wooden steps onto *Invincible* and were led to the Admiral's cabin for a private twenty-minute reunion with Prince Andrew. For all the royal party's outward calm, the Queen's decorous appearance Duke's Admiral of the Fleet uniform, the meeting must ha been intensely emotional, bu

The public facade was quickly regained for the photocall on one of the ship's decks (above) and the slow progress, as the last of the morning mists cleared, into harbour. Prince Andrew took the Press toward his helicopter (right) and was soon chatting freely about his adventures. He admitted feeling "different" after experiencing war at first hand. "I think my life has gone round the corner since I left one and a half months ago," he said. He had got on well with his companions – they proved it

by some good natured heckling as he spoke. "I couldn't forget this lot," he smiled. "They're an absolutely fantastic bunch. I would gladly keep going – particularly with this ship's company and the men I have served with in the Falklands." With just an inkling of the noises and the sights which lay immediately ahead of him and his ship, the war and its aftermath may have seemed a long way off, but there was time for a spot of self-analysis. "I felt lonely more than anything else," he confessed. "When you are down on the deck, when there are missiles flying around, then at that precise moment you are on your own and that's all there is. On the odd occasion I was terrified. To overcome fear I tried to adopt a positive mental attitude. I can't actually remember what I thought of – what I put in my mind – but I just remember telling myself 'I am going to survive this.'"

Survive he did, as did a crew of almost a thousand souls. Ahead of them lay Portsmouth harbour, busy with the unceasing movement of 55,000 relatives and friends anxious for the first sight of their loved ones. Half an hour after mid-day, the ship's

giving a rose to every returning crew member on the *Canberra,* the *Queen Elizabeth 2* and the *Hermes* in the previous three months. Perversely, it might seem, the public concentration on Prince Andrew, understandable though it was, was not particularly welcomed by the Prince himself. While he and the Queen were responding to calls from the crowds of "Well done, Mum, we're glad Andy's home," the appearance of a couple of private detectives, and of a Palace footman who came to pick up his baggage with its blue pointed labels from the single-berth cabin that had been his for almost six months, reminded him that royal rank would re-form the barrier which life

among his shipmates had effectively broken down. Well might he have thought – to paraphrase Queen Mary in 1945 – "Here I've been anybody to everybody, and back in London I shall have to begin being Prince Andrew all over again!" What he did say, more simply, was, "I'm not looking forward to going back to being a Prince. I'm a pilot."

"Being a Prince" started immediately. He was back in the world of public relations and walkabouts. The Queen and Prince Philip had agreed to see some of the thousands of other relatives crowding the quayside, and for a hundred yards they chatted casually with many of them. Prince Andrew was, of

Swordfish bi-planes performed the Royal Navy's own fly-past in honour of its heroes, and crews of ships from other NATO countries – Belgium, the Netherlands and Western Germany – joined in the celebrations. The dockside was itself a sea of faces – some cheering, some weeping, all searching – and of a multiplicity of banners identifying by name those who would be as welcome in their own parishes as Prince Andrew on a day when all *Invincible's* sailors were equal. But, of course, attention still focused on the royal crew member, and the public delight when he was presented with a long-stemmed red rose by 10-year-old Mandy Blythe was exceeded only when he voluntarily stuck it between his teeth for all to see (above). Then he removed the rose from his mouth with one hand, snatched off his white-topped cap with the other, and waved it high as he leapt into the air in a gesture of unrestrained joy and relief. The Queen, though more circumspect about her reactions, was equally delighted and certainly amused by the presentation to her of a single rose and a basket of red roses by the patriotically-dressed David Connolly (opposite page, bottom right), a florist from Croydon who was responsible for

...ines were shut off and in ...ght sunshine a host of small ...ts of all descriptions ...tled towards *Invincible's* ...n. On the quayside official ...ds struck up with tunes as ...ounding as *Rule Britannia* and ...d of Hope and Glory, and as ...sy as *Congratulations.* The ...ds weighed in, and the ...ors lining the rails of ...ncible couldn't resist ...ng in as well. At a signal ...0 red, white and blue ...oons were sent soaring into ...air, quickly gaining height ...floating off as little dark ... Coloured smoke was ...ultaneously released from ...sters, sirens shrieked, tugs ...ted fountains of water, a ...ation of historical

course, constrained to join in and with his ready reputation as a lady's man – he had been rumoured to have written letters to several girl friends during his absence – there was no shortage of requests from young ladies for a quick embrace. He refused, though tactfully, on the ground that "If I kissed you, I would have to kiss all the girls." The Queen was comparing notes with another mother, who confessed herself constantly worried for her son's safety. "I know how you felt," replied the Queen. "It's wonderful to have Andrew home." Home was not very far away. The Queen, Prince Philip and Princess Anne, having met their own family member and shared in the greetings for a thousand others, left the bustling, noisy harbour and its occupants to the joys of their own reunions.

Prince Andrew left with them, but made his way to London for the evening before returning to Portsmouth to fly his helicopter back to its base at RNAF Culdrose in Cornwall. There, a champagne celebration awaited him and other members of 820 Squadron – in spite of the Prince's own admission, at Portsmouth, that what he really looked forward to was a pint. "Of what?" he was asked. "Of milk. We haven't had any real milk for months." From Culdrose on the evening of 18th September, he flew to Balmoral to rejoin his parents, his

18th October, it was the end of what he described as "one hell of an experience." Not surprisingly, the Queen chose a photograph of him with his helicopter for her personal Christmas cards that December.

...ther the Prince of Wales, and ...Princess of Wales who was ...back from Monte Carlo where ...had been attending Princess ...ce's funeral.

...itically, economically and ...ially the effects of the ...paratively short Falklands ...mish were, and are, ...tinuing, wide-ranging, and ...subject of furious debate ...enquiry. Even the ...brations were not over – a ...sive military parade was held ...ondon the following October ...d the sadness and waste had ...not fully sunk in: that ...ld happen when the container-...s of coffins sent from ...ide early in September ...ght back the human cost of ...e. But *Invincible's* return ...he last of the great ...phant homecomings, and for ...ce Andrew and his ...agues, happily anticipating ...nth's shore leave before ...ting back to Culdrose on

The Queen closed the Commonwealth Games on 9th October and the competitions seemed almost incidental by then. In a thrilling afternoon's finals England, thanks partly to a wonderful 1,500 metre run by Steve Cram (above), nudged Australia off the top of the overall medals table. Keith Connor's triple jump was the second longest in history. Raelene Boyle retired amid unending praise and applause. The day's weather, performance and spirit were perfect. The Queen had time to enjoy it – and record it (right) – before pronouncing the closing words (above left). Matilda, winking coquettishly at all and sundry, was the most popular feature, even when swathed in coloured smoke from the Chinese dragon (left). The Queen even told her driver to slow down for her own final lap of honour.

On the evening of 10th October, the Governor-General of Australia, Sir Ninian Stephen and his wife, seen (opposite page, below) standing between Prince Philip and the Queen, gave a dinner at Government House, attended also by Mr and Mrs Malcom Fraser. On 11th October the royal visitors flew to Mount Druitt to open a new hospital which serves a large dormitory area for Sydney. It took its first patients during

I think she ought to bottle it." From Mount Druitt the Queen and Duke flew to Bathurst, a visit arranged at the Queen's request: she had not been there since 1954 and wanted to meet its people again. They turned out in their thousands to line the long, wide streets as she drove and walked to the City Hall for a State reception (remaining pictures).

previous month and the Queen and Duke were able to tour the wards, talking with working staff and with patients (below). The Duke had a few jovially sharp comments about hospital food, compulsory prayers and the illegibility of doctors' handwriting, but the Queen cheered up one patient, Mrs Dorothy Hilmer, handsomely: "She looked so young, she has a warmth about her, so friendly. The best medicine I've ever had.

drummers and bag-pipers in blue shirts and dark blue wraps bearing a bright orange bird of paradise design, played them into the inspection of the guard of honour (bottom right). Gun salutes drew whoops of surprise from the vast crowd sweltering in the heat, patiently awaiting

something on the lines of a walkabout – but there was none. Within a short time the royal party was on the long, winding road to Port Moresby's Hubert Murray Stadium, passing endless lines of people standing

e Queen and Prince Philip
ived in the land of almost a
usand languages when a Royal
stralian Air Force plane
ught them from Canberra to
t Moresby, capital of Papua
w Guinea, in the early
rnoon of 13th October. Over
languages and 400 dialects
spoken in this heavily
al country, though on
asions like this they all
n to fall silent. The Queen
Duke were welcomed by a
e-uniformed Governor-General
ow) as a band of pipers,

hair, along with the odd hibiscus bloom or circlet of frangipani. With the memory of the excitable children of Canberra still fresh, the comparative silence was eerie. Yet the sentiment was clear, epitomised by one banner sporting the first example of pidgin-English the Queen may have seen that day: "Welcum Misis Kwin Anytime."

That evening the Queen and Prince Philip were guests at a State dinner given by the Prime Minister Mr Somare (below) at

which 160 guests were present. The hotel selected for this occasion – the Papua Hotel – was an unpretentious one as, in an attempt not to overstrain National resources, a balance had to be achieved between luxury and cost. Almost in keeping with that concept, the guests were not all decked out in dinner jacket and black tie. Some of the men wore the skirt common to the South Pacific Islands, others wore lounge suits and ties, others wore open-necked shirts and slacks, and the variety of footwear was equally comprehensive. But it was a gratifyingly informal sort of State dinner for which the Queen, who had seemed to flag earlier in the day, may well have been grateful. A modest menu comprised chilled avoca

shoulder to shoulder and often four or five deep. Most held flags of independent Papua New Guinea in brilliant red, yellow and black; many waved them and a few had acquired Union Jacks as well. For some it was enough to stick them upright in their

and tomato soup, noisette of lamb with local vegetables and salad, orange and passion fruit mousse and Highlands coffee Papua Highlands, that is, not Scottish. And the wines were Australian.

On their first afternoon in Papua New Guinea, the Queen and Prince Philip were entertained at the Hubert Murray Stadium by a tribal carnival drawn from all over the country's lowlands.

Thirty thousand people had packed the stadium to see the royal party arrive to the rhythmic beating of welcoming drums.

Magnificent head-dresses stood four and five feet high, bristling with feathers of every conceivable indigenous bird but, proudest of all, with the much prized plumes of the dozens of species of bird of paradise. Protected by law, they may be captured only for the use of their feathers in head-dresses, which become priceless tribal heirlooms. Grass skirts, beautifully fashioned, abounded, as did festoons of horn necklaces and hosts of baubles symbolic of wealth or rank. The dancing seemed to go on for ever, several groups in various parts of the huge field performing simultaneously, none stopping without another taking up. The continuous throb of tom-toms quickened and slowed the pace of ritual movements, stout poles hung with shells were banged on the ground to induce changes of tempo, and all the while the small armies of dancers charged, bobbed, swung

and gyrated until, almost perversely, a band from the Royal Yacht *Britannia,* pith-helmeted and red-sashed, were marched on to herald the Queen departure. For once their polished excellence was swamp by the burnished, primitive splendour around them.
The following day the Queen a

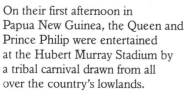

Prince Philip flew to Mount Hagen in the Papuan Highlands to watch a sing-sing – a festival of song and dance, very similar to that given at Port Moresby, but pertaining to tribal life in the highlands. Communities had been on the march for days to be here, and the day had been declared an "amnesty day" when, in this tribally hostile region, bows and arrows may not be

carried except for cultural purposes. Here again was a vast assembly of scores of tribes, painted and dressed a hundred different ways (overleaf) and limbering up to give their best performance for Misis Kwin and for Man Bilong Kwin.

But it all went horribly wrong. As the Queen arrived, a storm was already gathering. As she and Prince Philip drove around the enclosure many dancers, fearing for their precious head-

gear, were fleeing, and droves of spectators followed them as the elegant royal thrones on the thatch-covered podium were filled. The rain started as the Queen began her reply to the Premier's speech of welcome; a clap of thunder marked its conclusion, and when the Queen looked up only a handful of people met her gaze. The full fury of an icy cold storm followed and the royal party beat a hasty retreat back to Mount Hagen airport and thence to the scorching heat of the capital.

The Royal Yacht *Britannia* took the Queen and Prince Philip from Port Moresby to the Solomon Islands, giving them the agreeable bonus of three days' relaxation as they neared the Equator. Early in the morning of 18th October, the Yacht anchored off-shore and the royal barge brought the travellers (opposite page, bottom left) to

fish casually swimming in the harbour's clear pool.

The guard was duly inspected (opposite page, top left), the local dignitaries duly introduced (left) and the royal party taken to Lawson Tama, a large recreation stadium in Honiara where the sound of the conch shell and a fierce but traditional warrior challenge heralded their arrival. Here they watched a succession of

Honiara harbour. The far quayside was thick with spectators who covered four wide jetties, climbed every tree and waded as far as necessary into the water to see the proceedings. Umbrellas were put to good use (left) as a brilliant sun shot the temperature into the thirties – even at 9.30 in the morning – and illuminated the bright colours of the numerous parrot

...es by groups from the us Solomon Islands, and ...cted displays of local ...re and handicrafts – ...erware, the making of shell ...y, canoe manufacture and ...chold interests. The Queen ... under a white parasol, ...or her by a local official ...osite page, bottom right) as ...plied, thanking the ...ers for their gifts of ... carvings and for the star ... Solomon Islands she had ...ceived as the first ...nt of the highest of the ...ls' honours. It was a ...drive to the Central

Hospital, whose open-air corridors were beautifully decked out with flowers and bunting (opposite page, top right) and smelled of frangipani and hibiscus. The Queen was in her element as she visited the maternity wards, but the Duke came away less pleased. He had been told that the Islands' population growth rate was almost 5% – the highest in the South Pacific. He warned that "in twenty years' time there will be an economic crisis and you'll be blaming it on everyone else." "Five per cent!" he muttered to himself. "They must

be out of their minds!" Pointedly he did not rejoin the Queen for the remainder of her tour of the maternity unit. Babies appearing at that rate had clearly lost their appeal.

The Queen had changed into a
cool, blue outfit with a
flamboyant feather-trimmed hat
for the visit to the National
Museum late that afternoon.
Here she and Prince Philip saw
an exhibition of the history of
the Islands before they became a
British protectorate – a period

pleased to see activities
connected with his Award Scheme.
At the National Archives the
Queen and Prince Philip toured
an exhibition of wartime
photographs and met five
veterans (left) of the fierce
fighting to defend the Solomons.

ingly referred to as
"omon Time Before." From
they passed through a
oo grove into Coronation
ens, where the children's
awaited them. The Queen
ved a bouquet from four-
old Indy Tapalia – Indy
short for Independence,
she was born on Solomons'
endence Day in 1978 – and
to several groups of
s, Guides and primary and
dary school children (far
. The Duke was a great
rite (above) and was

The mid-point of a tour of exciting and sometimes refreshingly primitive island communities, the royal visit to Nauru was certainly the most thought-provoking. Nauru is only eight square miles in area and produces nothing save phosphate. Mined continuously since the 1890s, the phosphate supply is now close to exhaustion.

The Queen's welcome on her arrival from *Britannia* by barge

(below and opposite page) was as genuine as any, yet there was a strangeness in the surroundings. The red carpet she set foot on was imported from New Zealand; the 30-strong school band which struck up the National Anthems on her arrival and serenaded her through the day, had been flown in from Melbourne; the management and supervisory staff of the phosphate mines, which the royal couple toured, were English and Australian; the dancers who entertained them at

a garden party that afternoon were from Western Samoa, Kiribati, Tuvala – anywhere, it seemed, but from Nauru. Even the handsomely-decorated coffee table, inlaid with the Star of Nauru in phosphate rock, and standing on carved lion's foot legs – presented to the Queen during the official farewells (far left) – was tactfully described as "Made under the supervision of Nauruans."

sunshine.

The day was punctuated by ceremonies in maneabas, or meeting houses, where hono[u]r the form of plaited cords (far left) and dried-leaf garlands (below) were bestowed, and

Iosiabata was the name of the man brought from Maina Island to Kiribati's capital Tarawa, to ensure good weather for the Queen's visit on 23rd October. He justified the cost of his passage and food. As the Queen arrived, the early morning rains stopped, leaving the remainder of the day bathed in hot

the drinking of coconut water straight from the shell was as much a ritual as an opportunity for refreshment. Shortly before the Queen arrived, the tin roof of a house gave way under the weight of dozens of people using it as a vantage point. On the island of Betio that afternoon, the branch of a tree followed suit, when it became over-loaded with sightseers.

Prince Philip, accompanying the Queen to Tarawa's Tungaru Hospital (opposite page, top right) lapsed into chatty informality in no time. Told of the number of injuries caused by drunken drivers, he said, "I'm not surprised, judging by the quantity of empty beer cans around the island. You really ought to get someone to clear up the empties."

After a colourful parade of local schoolchildren at Tarawa's

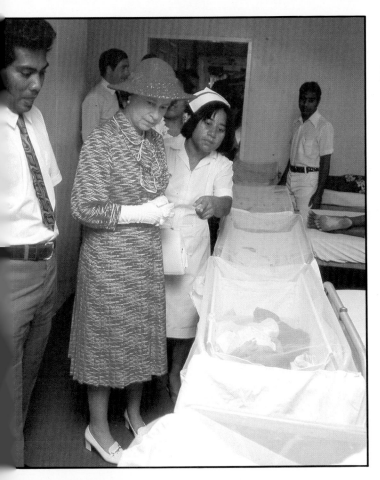

rts field (left) and a superb
n-air lunch in the gardens of
e House, close by one of
wa's long, wide beaches, the
en and the Duke sailed for
o where they separated – the
en to see a display of
ge technology, the Duke to
ct a marine Training School
(facing page,top) find time
nother quick drink. They
again in the Island's
eaba for a magnificent
ering of traditional songs
to receive gifts before
ng for Tuvalu.

it's Tuesday, it must be
...valu," was certainly not one
...the Queen's thoughts as she
...proached the island of
...nafuti, capital of the former
...ce Islands. In a life where
...well-prepared and even the
...ectacular may seem routine,
...re was nothing remotely
...undane about the start – nor
...eed the end – of her two-day
...t, beginning on 26th October
...Tuvalu. There is a harbour
...e, and the royal barge might
...e used it, but conditions
...e good enough for a more
...inctive welcome. The barge
...met by a flotilla of long
...bes, whose paddlers were
...rged with the duty of
...veying the Queen, Prince
...ip and their party to the
...re (opposite page, top). The
...bes – built in a week, of
...t hardwood called puka, and
...ing no more than $270

(about £150) – were
copies of those used locally for
skipjack fishing, but the bright
colours of protective paint
marked their special purpose
today.

That night the celebrations continued. The Queen and Prince Philip were back in the maneapa for a traditional feast, served in an equally traditional manner. In a carefully rehearsed procession, bearers brought an amazing selection of food – legs of pork, quarters of chicken, crabs, lobsters and fish, even cooked blackbirds and bats, a whole succession of vegetables and fruit from the huge taros, or sweet potatoes, to the clusters of small bananas. The

Queen was visibly uncertain how to tackle this enormous spread, and seemed self-consciously to inspect and study its constituents, rather than to taste them. Prince Philip had no such reservations, and joked happily with his serving girl as he tucked into a variety of dishes. Afterwards, a ceremonial crowning, in which all the guests received decorative circlets of flowers, left the Queen with a cluster of densely arranged frangipani on her head, and the Duke with a more rakish version of straw and flame tree blooms on his – a result at which the Duke was openly amused (opposite page). This ceremony heralded the beginning of the evening's entertainment, and the Queen and Prince Philip moved from this table (far right) to watch a three-hour programme of non-stop singing. Every one of Tuvalu's

nine little islands was represented: singers from each community performing three or four songs – some of welcome, others of island legends, others versifying modern events like World War II battles, and the Apollo moon missions.

The Queen and Duke left by the same route and in the same manner as they had come. Only the warm, saturating rain and the noticeable, underlying sadness of departure distinguished the two events. Anticipating the rain, the Queen had her transparent umbrella ready, but her hosts had provided a much more colourful substitute.

"Tuvalu," the Prime Minister had told the Queen, "has little in the way of land or natural resources, but we believe we have a happiness, culture and friendliness which are perhaps more important than pure material wealth." No-one who spent those two days on Funafuti could possibly doubt the truth of the assertion. Those qualities were evident everywhere and always, making Tuvalu one country at least that the Queen must have been genuinely sorry to leave.

attempt to outshine her hosts, she chose a subdued yet elegant cerise evening dress with just a fraction of the sparkle sported by the Pearly folk and showed that, within sight of her 81st birthday and despite, as she herself admits, "failing in sight and limbs," she can still command respect as one of the most poised members of the Royal Family.

The Pearlies, quintessential representatives of the Cockneys whose affection for the Royal Family is well known, presented Princess Alice not only with a

Like her son and daughter-in-law, Princess Alice Duchess of Gloucester is a regular visitor to major farming exhibitions, and her presence on 6th July at the Royal Show at Stoneleigh (above and top) was the continuation of a practice which is perhaps almost taken for granted. After a two-month summer break, Princess Alice's official diary began in earnest with a visit to County Hall in London to attend the Pearly Kings' and Queens' annual charity ball on 1st October (opposite page). Eschewing flamboyance herself, and in any event wisely deciding not to

bouquet of freesias and asters (opposite page, centre) but also with a Pearly doll (opposite page, bottom right) which has no doubt found its way into the hands of one or both of her grand-daughters, Lady Davina and Lady Rose Windsor.

Her second engagement of the autumn, on 11th October, involved a short trip from her London home at Kensington Palace to the Royal Albert Hall, to watch a gala of Gilbert and Sullivan operas – where else to meet the Yeoman of the Guard? (right) – presented by Solid Rock Foundation in aid of the Mental Health Foundation and the

D'Oyly Carte Opera Trust. Princess Alice was at this time putting the finishing touches to her memoirs, but in the meantime one of her former butlers, Peter Russell, had published his own highly entertaining – if on the face of it a trifle far-fetched – anecdotal memoirs, *Butler Royal.* They confirmed the generally held view that the late Duke had a temper worthy of any military man, but that Princess Alice soon learned how to draw upon her reserves of resourcefulness and determination to circumvent it.

When you are a major fashion show's guest of honour among 600 connoisseurs of Western chic, your entrance has to be spectacular. So on 9th November, while the Prince of Wales was tramping his estates in Cornwall, his wife put on her latest and most fetching evening dress for her visit to the Guildhall in London, where the charity Birthright was able to raise £30,000 gross towards funds for their research into the problems of childbirth. Preceded by a dinner, the show, organized by the Princess'

fashion advisor Anna Harvey, consisted of over a hundred British, and a few additional French designs, from the ornate in gold-embroidered ball gowns to the less simple allurements of plastic-boned bodices. Many of the Princess' own favourite designers were among the exhibitors. Unfortunately, Diana's slim look rebounded on her. Within a week she was widely and persistently rumoured to have contracted anorexia nervosa, the slimmers' disease which can cause death. Aware that her sister, Lady Sarah McCorquodale was once a victim, and that the disease is hereditary, a public genuinely anxious about the extremes to which the Princess appeared to be going to regain her shape after Prince William's birth was fed graphic newspaper accounts of her supposed decline. Palace denials did not convince many – and still have not – that she was at that time enjoying normal health.

called Valentine, to add to her already impressive possessions at the royal stables (left). Prince Claus' illness forced him to miss some engagements, but was a smiling farewell for all on 19th November (right).

Eight members of the Royal Family were at Westminster Pier on 16th November to welcome Queen Beatrix and Prince Claus of the Netherlands for a four-day State visit. The visitors' arrival followed a trip in the ceremonial barge *Royal Nore* from Greenwich, where they were met by the Prince of Wales. In the customary exchange of gifts, Queen Elizabeth received a horse

After the explosion of reportage on the subject of Prince Andrew's exploits with the actress Koo Stark, it was inevitable that he should be mobbed by a crowd of young girls on one of his rare public engagements. On 18th November, he was invited to switch on the Christmas lights in Regent Street. The rush to see the Prince gave the police a difficult job, but female screams were hushed long enough for him to complete the ceremony and say a few words. He referred to the long-held belief that Christmas trees – the theme of the illuminations – were introduced into England by the Prince Consort, and as he threw the switch he said, "I'm told there are 55,000 bulbs in those Christmas trees. I just hope they all work." Give or take one or two, they did and the Prince then attended a reception (these pages) given by the Regent Street Association.

Rarely do the Prince and
Princess of Wales miss an
opportunity to assist with fund-
raising for the Mountbatten
Memorial Trust, and the European
premiere of *Gandhi,* held amid
enormous publicity at the Odeon
Theatre in London's Leicester
Square, was a case in point.
Countess Mountbatten was there,
as was Barbara Cartland,
together with a galaxy of
international film celebrities,
and those directly connected
with the film – Sir Richard
Attenborough, Sir John Gielgud,
Sir John Mills and Ben Kingsley.
The Prince and Princess'
entrance was impressive, the
Princess re-calling one of the
most elegant gowns of her 1981
wardrobe. Prince Charles was

quietly satisfied with all he
saw and heard, as everyone
craned their necks for a glimps
of his glittering wife. She
suffered from the intense heat
of the brilliant television
lights – "If you stand here lon;
enough, you nearly pass out,"
she said during another premi
six months later. And this
occasion failed to pass withou
a reference to Prince William
"He never stops eating," the
Princess told Sir John Mills.

sunlit morning of 6th December he joined the Quorn hunt for a chase over the snow covered countryside near Melton Mowbray in Leicestershire. The outing – the Prince was unaccompanied by his wife – did nothing to stem yet another newspaper report that their sixteen-month-old marriage was in difficulties. The *Daily Mail's* gossip columnist, Nigel Dempster, added fuel to that particular fire when, in an interview on American television, he branded the Princess of Wales a "fiend" who "is very much ruling the roost" and making Prince Charles "desperately unhappy". In Britain, Dempster refused to withdraw, on the grounds that if the Princess was "making the Prince unhappy, we should know about it." Buckingham Palace condemned the comments as "totally stupid" and revealed that the Princess was "very upset" by them.

Princess Anne, the Prince
Wales has become a devotee of
unting, and has attracted
ir share of critics for
g so. They failed to
ade him when, on the crisp,

sunlit morning of 6th December he joined the Quorn hunt for a chase over the snow covered countryside near Melton Mowbray in Leicestershire. The outing – the Prince was unaccompanied by his wife – did nothing to stem yet another newspaper report that their sixteen-month-old marriage was in difficulties. The *Daily Mail's* gossip columnist, Nigel Dempster, added fuel to that particular fire when, in an interview on American television, he branded the Princess of Wales a "fiend" who "is very much ruling the roost" and making Prince Charles "desperately unhappy". In Britain, Dempster refused to withdraw, on the grounds that if the Princess was "making the Prince unhappy, we should know about it." Buckingham Palace condemned the comments as "totally stupid" and revealed that the Princess was "very upset" by them.

Princess Anne, the Prince [of W]ales has become a devotee of [h]unting, and has attracted [the]ir share of critics for [doing] so. They failed to [persu]ade him when, on the crisp,

Barbican Theatre. The choice of play was no coincidence. Almost fifty years before, its author J. M. Barrie bequeathed the royalties from his book to the Great Ormond Street Hospital. Now under severe financial strictures, the hospital was grateful for the capital asset and royal support.

The Great Ormond Street Hospital for Sick Children made the most of its royal patronage in December. On the 2nd, the Princess of Wales visited the hospital amid a great show of popularity from nursing and administration staff. On 15th December, the Queen, who is the hospital's patron, attended a performance (these pages) of the Royal Shakespeare Company's new production of *Peter Pan* at the

With the approach of Christmas, the inevitable party season got under way, and the Royal Family were not left out. On 16th December Princess Michael of Kent went to East London to attend a Christmas party at Wanstead Almshouses (bottom left). A week beforehand her brother-in-law the Duke of Kent attended a Variety Club lunch with a particularly Christmas flavour about it. Staged at the London Hilton Hotel, the lunch marked the end of the Club's Christmas toy campaign in which 20,000 toys were distributed to

sick and deprived children throughout the country. It also featured the Variety Club's famous "Miss Christmases", drawn from the casts of musicals *Song and Dance* and *Cats*: they are seen (top right) with the Duke

at the pre-lunch reception. After the lunch, the Duke received a cheque for the RNLI, of which he is President, and which saved no fewer that 1,281 lives at sea in 1982.

The Duchess of Kent, meanwhile, kept a regular annual Christmas appointment by attending the Not Forgotten Association's Christmas party, held at the Royal Riding Stables at Buckingham Palace (pictures above). Publicity tends to be concentrated on the Association's older members, particularly the Chelsea Pensioners, but recent campaigns continue to result in many younger men and women benefiting from its efforts. The MP Hugh Rossi told an audience of 350 at the party that there were now over a quarter of a million disabled war pensioners, with ages ranging from 25 to over 100.

One of the oldest, 101-year-old

courage it can inspire made her encounter with fourteen children a moving experience. She was there to present the annual Children of Courage Awards (above, below and left), and to make the acquaintance of children who had overcome cancer, bone disease, brain damage and blindness to live active, useful lives. Others had performed mountain rescues, chased burglars and saved friends from collapsing masonry. Their citations were read out during the presentation ceremony, and the Queen Mother gave each an award – in the shape of a bird set in perspex – and a citation scroll. Then, in front of a Christmas tree in the Deanery Courtyard, they all posed with her for a photograph to commemorate a pleasant finale to an exciting year.

derick Page, who served in
ia and lost an eye at the
denelles, shared the
monial knife with the
hess of Kent as this year's
e was cut. Baked by the Army
ring Corps, the cake was
with a replica of the
ciation's badge. Like that
e Duchess' left lapel, it
ed the head of an elephant.
atron of the Spastics
ety, the Duchess was present
days later (left) at the
national Show Jumping
npionships at Olympia in aid
e Stars' Association for
tics.
catalogue of misfortune
g the Queen Mother to
minster Abbey on 15th
mber is hardly the stuff of
Christmas is made, but the

Prince William (previous pages), was among four royal infants absent from Christmas Day mattins at St George's Chapel. But, excepting Prince Edward and the Queen Mother, everyone else attended. Less familiar faces included Captain Phillips with son Peter (right) and the Kent children Nicholas, Helen and George talking to Viscount Linley and his sister Sarah (bottom right).

RAF Benson has received many royal visitors; the Queen's Flight, established by King Edward VIII in 1936 at Hendon, has been based there continuously for 37 years, and Prince Edward gained his glider's wings there in 1980. On 12th January Princess Alexandra – equal first with the Duke of Gloucester for performing the first royal public engagement of 1983 – paid a four-hour visit to the base. Elegantly and well wrapped up against a bleak winter's day, her first job was to join the officers of the Queen's Flight for a group photograph (below). A forty-minute inspection of the Queen's Flight followed, before the Princess was taken to the sergeants' mess for a reception at which she signed the visitors' book. Luncheon at the officers' mess was taken to the

accompaniment of a selection of waltzes and film themes played by the Salon Orchestra of the Central Band of the RAF. During the afternoon, the Princess toured the station's twelve-roomed sports pavilion, and the education section where she met some of the families of RAF

personnel at an informal, hour-long tea party.
(Above and top) Princess Alexandra, who is patron of the English National Opera Company, visited its rehearsal and production centre at Lilian Baylis House in Hampstead on 25th January.

Royalty from Britain and Spain met on 13th January when a tercentenary exhibition of paintings by the Spanish artist Murillo opened at the Royal Academy of Arts in London. The Duke and Duchess of Gloucester (below) arrived first, five minutes before Queen Sophie of Spain.

oyal Academy of Arts again
ained royalty when the
and Princess of Wales
ed a reception (left) in
ction with "Britain Salutes
ork" – a festival marking
centenary of the end of
merican War of
endence. This was the
and Princess' first
engagement since their
ut eventful, far-from-
holiday in Liechtenstein
sts of that principality's
parent Prince Hans Adam.
Charles and his wife
had a chance to avoid the
ons of photographers,
British and continental,
e entire holiday of just
an a week was ruined by
d-mouse tactics. After

some pretty harsh words from the
Prince's detective, the British
press cried off, but the foreign
contingent was not so easily
deterred. In the event it was
surprising that the royal couple
were in a mood to smile at all
when they got back to London.
The Duke of Kent was luckier.
He went off on 20th January to
Sestriere in Northern Italy to
attend the Kandahar/Martini
International Ski-ing
Championships, and was able to
find time to keep up his ski-ing
practice in between attending
receptions and awarding prizes
during the five-day event
(remaining pictures). Unlike
January 1982 at Meribel, in
France, his family did not
accompany him.

was a little late for
[V]alentine's Day, but as it was
[ju]st over two years to the day
[sin]ce her engagement, the
[Pr]incess of Wales might have
[th]ought the heart-shaped bouquet
[(ab]ove) appropriate as she began
[he]r visit to Brookfields School
[fo]r Mentally Handicapped
[Ch]ildren at Tilehurst on 25th
[Feb]ruary. "She's a natural,"
[wa]s the most often repeated
[co]mpliment. "I'd have her on my
[staf]f any day," added the
[sch]ool's headmaster.

western hemisphere she has ev
undertaken. The royal couple
arrived at Kingston, Jamaica
(top left) in scorching weather
which made sub-zero Britain s
light years away. The welcomir
procedures (far left) were as
standard as the following day's
cultural "Salute to the Queen"
was typically Jamaican. Scores

Just over three months after
landing in London from a month-
long tour of Australia and the
South Pacific, the Queen left
Heathrow Airport with Prince
Philip on 13th February for the
most extensive tour of the

Alexander Bustamente, preceded a medley of traditional folk tunes in celebration of Jamaica's twenty first year of independence. The Queen, showed genuine pleasure (left) at this

...ousands of almost ...ntrollable Jamaicans forgot ...everyday problems and put ...eir finest show of ...times almost delirious ...usiasm (top and far right). ...aginative parade of fifteen ...ical effigies, from ...topher Columbus to ...ca's first president, Sir

colourful show. "Every time Prince Philip and I come here," she told the Governor-General at a State banquet that evening, "you seem to have some special event to greet us."
Earlier that day she had been to Gordon House to address the Jamaican Parliament. She praised the country's

maintenance of democratic principles despite what she termed "pressures and strains that have stretched its social fabric" – a reference to a period of tumultuous and bloody unrest at the time of the 1980 elections, in which the former left-wing premier Michael Manley was defeated. His aspirations

to turn the country into a republic were thought to have been effectively put in their place by the Queen's reference to herself as "Queen of Jamaica," but in fact this is her common practice in all countries acknowledging her as sovereign. A walkabout afterwards (bottom right) showed she certainly enjoyed great popular support.

On 15th February the Queen and Duke visited Montego Bay, and saw twelve thousand people packed into Sam Sharpe Square as she attended a civic reception (below) and watched a march past (opposite page).

It is said that the invitation for the Queen and Prince Philip to visit California was made on horseback, while Her Majesty and President Ronald Reagan took their celebrated early-morning canter through Windsor Great Park in June 1982.

The Queen and Duke arrived in San Diego on 26th February, and another memorable chapter began. And it began in style, with official ceremony (below and opposite page, top), followed by a trip round San Diego harbour to review a small section of America's mighty Navy, and a visit to the aircraft-carrier USS *Ranger* to

inspect some of the fighter and anti-submarine planes on board (top left and opposite page, below). With an appreciative eye towards blending the old a the new, the Queen and Prince Philip heard a recital of Shakespeare at the Old Globe Theatre, and visited the huge Scripps Institute of Oceanography – 230 acres of insight into the geological and biological secrets of earth, ocean and atmosphere. The D admired the technology but perhaps, like most of us, the Queen was more readily attrac to the more understandable achievements of intelligent marine life (left).

– though nothing like it would be in the days to come. That evening saw probably the most publicised royal event since the Coronation. At the studios of Twentieth Century Fox at Long Beach a dinner, billed by some quirk of understatement as Hollywood's social event of the year, brought together the Queen, her husband and 500 guests comprising the royalty of the film world. Mrs Nancy Reagan hosted the event and escorted the Queen into the midst of that film world's distinguished company – Frank Sinatra, Perry Como, George

ay 27th February was more
ed, with a single morning's
gement in the form of
ns at St Paul's Episcopal
ch (these pages). The
er gave ample notice of its
ions: for the second day
dull and threatened rain

Burns, James Stewart, Michael Caine, Elton John, Fred Astaire, Rod Stewart and Dudley Moore to name but a very small section. For all the outward confidence, there was confusion in the ranks. The evening did not get off to the best start; partly because of the atrocious weather outside, partly because a group of fifty pro-IRA demonstrators heckled the Queen and Prince Philip as they arrived. Inside, meanwhile, the invitations specifying informal dress had put everyone into a quandary over balancing informality and respect. Dudley Moore spilt soup onto his trousers in the Duke's presence. Even Mrs Reagan confessed, rather shakily, that this was the first event she had ever hosted alone. There was also a whiff of offence. Many American stars had been placed too far away

from the Queen and Prince Philip at the top table ever to have a chance to speak with them. They argued afterwards – and some of the British stars agreed with them – that the Queen could meet her own countrymen anytime: this was an occasion when Americans should have pride of place. But the Queen apparently had wished it otherwise and

Michael Caine was her nearest, and very British fellow guest. For all that the show went without any obvious hitch. George Burns put on his famous drawling act of desultory monologue. Frank Sinatra and Perry Como sang – rather too lengthily, and badly under-rehearsed thought Elton John – and Dionne Warwick raised the

of with a medley of popular
numbers. Some of the tributes
to the Queen tended to ooze with
Hollywood's traditional
fulsomeness – a characteristic
which the Queen herself found
somewhat amusing. But she
enjoyed the entertainment as a
whole, clapping in time with
many of the songs, while Prince
Philip chuckled away at George
Burns' jokes, both old and new.
The cynics wondered who
wouldn't, after a sumptuous meal
of papaya with bay shrimp,
chicken pot pie, fresh spinach
with bacon, toasted coconut ice-
cream snowballs and rivers of
Californian wines!

The first royal engagement of 28th February carried with it the risk that Prince Philip would upstage the Queen. The venue was the Rockwell International Corporation – the home of the American space shuttle – where a simulator was ready for inspection in the mock-up chamber. The Queen

entered the module first (far left) and activated the automatic pilot to simulate a descent to earth at over 400 miles an hour from 10,000 feet Prince Philip's turn came, and with an expert's eye "took" the craft down from an even higher altitude. The Royal couple also saw the Apollo XIV command module, before being taken from the Centre to Los Angeles City Hall for a reception. Yet another burst of rain delayed the Queen's motorcade by thirty minutes, and yet another band of Sinn Fein supporters jeered and chanted as she arrived.

Afterwards, the Queen and Prince Philip went to Los Angeles Music Center (these pages) for a lunch consisting of such exotic dishes as limestone lettuce salad, asparagus spears wrapped in red peppers, and lemon sorbet in whole fruit shell. The meal was preceded by a brief appearance on the balcony outside (opposite page, top right) and followed by the presentation of a hand-painted porcelain sculpture.

Plans for the Queen to sail in *Britannia* to Santa Barbara on 1st March were scuppered by storms which put the city's harbour out of action, and she and Prince Philip had to fly from Long Beach to rejoin the Reagans, who were by now beginning to feel personally apologetic for the continuing bad weather. Their arrival was attended by all the hastily-prepared ritual of State – there followed a hazardous twenty-mile journey by car through the flooded roads winding up to the Reagan's acre ranch in the Santa Ynez mountains.

The plans at the Reagan ranch fizzled out equally effectively. There was lunch of course, but the invitation to go riding – a reciprocal gesture for the amicable episode at Windsor nine months before – had to be called off in favour of a simple photo-call (left and right) for which neither hosts nor guests seemed to have much enthusiasm. There was no let up in the chaos caused by worsening rain during the following few days. Things reached an all time low when the Queen and Prince Philip were forced to book into a hotel in San Francisco on the night of 2nd March, instead of spending that night on board *Britannia*. But the following evening all seemed forgiven at the State dinner given by President Reagan at the de Young Memorial Museum. "I knew before we came," mused the Queen (below), "that we had exported many of our traditions to the United States. I had not realised that the weather was one of them."

After lunch at President Reagan's ranch on 1st March, Mrs Reagan took the Queen and Prince Philip to the Santa Barbara Mission, a capacious Latin-American-style church in warm cream and pink masonry, founded on St Barbara's Day, 1786. It has the unique distinction of being the sole survivor of twenty-one Californian missions built before 1823 as permanent homes for Franciscan padres, and it was the present incumbents who welcomed the small royal party to the building today (above). After touring the mission (top right), the Queen planted a tree in the grounds to commemorate her visit (bottom centre). The rain held off for that brief moment and the ubiquitous royal umbrella was not needed.

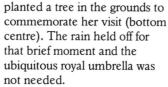

Of five engagements underta
on 3rd March, a king-sized
entertainment at the Sympho
Hall, (opposite page, top) ke
the Queen amused and delig
(above). Another involved a
visit to Hewlett Packard's
computer factory (top and fa
left). The following day the
Queen and Prince Philip gav
dinner on board *Britannia* to
celebrate the Reagans' 31st
wedding anniversary (right a
previous page).A more natu
grandeur characterised their
visit to the Yosemite Nation
Park on 5th March (overlea

The Legislative Buildings
(right) provided the background
for the welcoming salutes as the
Queen and Prince Philip arrived
at Victoria, British Columbia,
on 8th March. While *Britannia*
tied up at Ship Point (far
right) her barge (below) took
the Queen to dry land. The
inspection of the guard of
honour (opposite page, top left)
and the speeches were completed
under the threat or reality of
rain, but the warmth shown to
the Queen during her walkabout
afterwards (opposite page,
centre right) demonstrated that
her visit was long overdue.

The posy of spring flowers presented to the Queen (previous pages) by four-year-old Erin Johnson engaged a grateful royal smile at Victoria's City Hall. Here a civic welcome prefaced a royal walkabout from Centennial Square to the Gate of Harmonious Interest in the town's Chinese quarter, where the Queen and Prince Philip watched a lion

...nce and chatted to some of the ...inese population (opposite ...ge, bottom left). It was an ...ormously busy day. With two ...mal receptions behind them ...eady, the Queen and Duke gave ...ir own reception for members ...the press on board *Britannia*, ...fore lunching on chicken ...reme at the Empress Hotel. ...e afternoon's engagements ...luded a visit to Christ ...urch Cathedral, a tour of ...igflower School, recently ...ored, and tea at Royal Roads ...itary College, where 250 ...ets provided the guard of ...our (overleaf).

Britannia arrived in the impressive Vancouver Harbour 9th March to a welcome by Prime Minister Trudeau and a mass of balloons proclaiming "Canada With Love" (previous page). At the university of British Columbia a walkabout (these pages) linked a tour of the Museum, where Kwakiutl Indians danced for the Queen, and a visit to the Asian centre.
Spring flowers (right) suggested

a fitting tribute to fine spring weather – at last – and the Queen had a word for even the youngest Brownie to present her with an unofficial bouquet (opposite page). That afternoon the Queen and Duke were at the site of Expo '86. The Queen set the ball rolling by extending an invitation "to all peoples of the world from the people of Canada" to visit the Exposition in May 1986. And the British

Columbians were thrilled to learn later that the Prince and Princess of Wales would visit Vancouver to perform the opening ceremony.

Bristol Hospital for Sick Children's intensive care unit (above, left and below) but only the young patients enjoyed her company as she sat on their beds, watched them at play, and told them not to suck thumbs. And after visiting wards where children were suffering from cancer and leukemia, she was told by one her hosts, "I have never seen anyone establish a rapport with patients in the way you have." A month later, on 2nd March, she opened a £7 million shopping precinct in Aylesbury (opposite page and pictures far left) and was highly amused to discover a cosmetic called Starkers. "I didn't know they made nude make-up," she said.

ombination of the Princess
les and children in
tal brings out the best in
On 4th February, two
and people saw her open the

There were no surprise royal
visitors, and no surprise
absentees, at the Badminton
Horse Trials from 14th to 17
April. The Queen gave the e
the prestige it habitually
derives from her presence, m
to the evident satisfaction of
the Duke of Beaufort (below
celebrated his 83rd birthday
days beforehand. Prince and

Princess Michael (far left), active participants in hunting and point-to-points, attended again and the royal Phillipses were represented in full. Princess Anne, still trying desparately to bring on two young horses for eventing herself, watched the proceedings and carried her two-year-old daughter Zara around in between times, stopping for a quick look at a pair of draught horses (opposite page, top right). With them was five-year-old Peter, now in his second year at

Minchinhampton Blue Boys School. Lying sixth after the dressage – only 6.6 points behind the leader Mike Tucker of Dalwhinnie, Captain Phillips was forced to retire when his horse Classic Lines refused at the eleventh fence in the cross country, and threw its rider to the ground.

In a thrilling finish, it was Lucinda Green on Regal Realm who won for the fifth time. The Queen presented the Whitbread Trophy with the warm congratulations of a woman who appreciates good horsemanship. And, as usual (these pages), she was back on the Badminton estate on Sunday 17th April to attend the customary church service. She is seen (above) leaving Badminton House with the Duke of Beaufort, Prince Philip and Princess Anne that morning.

The army had its share of ro
favour during the year, too, a
the Queen Mother was a fre
guest of honour. On 10th M
she arrived at Colchester to
visit the Royal Anglian
Regiment. The weather pro
less welcoming than her hos
as she began her inspection

the six guards of honour, a
sudden downpour caught ev
unawares. She happily conti
her inspection (top left) befo
watching a parade (left) and
touring the Meeanee and
Hyderabad Barracks (above
opposite page, bottom right
Security was tight on this
occasion, but not nearly so
stringent as for her visit to
celebrate the 75th anniversa
of the Territorial Army in
Northern Ireland six weeks
later. Then, the Queen Moth
– who could well have justifi

staying at home – showed both personal courage and a confidence in the arrangements being made for her safety. A rash of bomb scares failed to deter her. Far from it: she fairly ambled through her schedule as if she were in the familiar surroundings of her own back garden. In so doing, she honoured her hosts, encouraged the local community and won for herself universal praise for putting duty first.

The Princess of Wales oozed confidence during her first public outing since returning from Australasia with Prince Charles. After her resounding success down-under, she was doing her favourite thing, making friends with the young. It was 13th May, and the

...rincess visited two centres for
...andicapped children – the
...loucestershire Adventure
...ayground at Coberley – where
...e picked up and cuddled five-
...ar-old Andrew Harrison, who
...n towards her with great
...citement – and Paradise House
...ollege at Painswick.

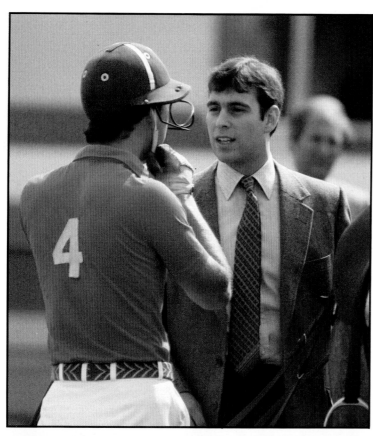

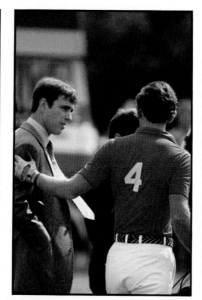

becomes almost newsworthy. Prince Andrew was at Smith's Lawn Windsor on 15th May to watch Prince Charles play in his first match since returning from Australasia, where he played three times and was on the winning side each time. Also present at Windsor were Lord a⎸ Lady Tryon, once fast friends of Prince Charles.

Prince Andrew, due to carry out solo engagements during his tim⎸ in Britain that summer, was allotted a private secretary, Squadron Leader Adam Wise, formerly the Queen's equerry, from the beginning of October.

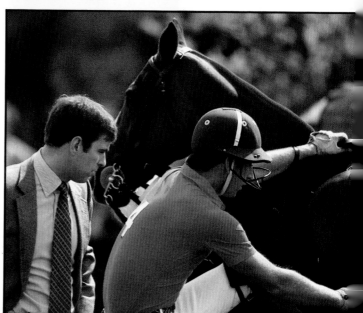

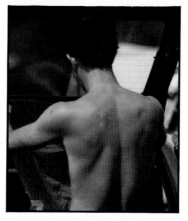

A spot of innocent horse-play never comes amiss, especially on the polo field, and when it develops between a couple of fun-loving brothers who happen to be first and third in succession to the Throne, it

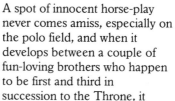

One event Princess Margaret rarely misses each year is the Royal Caledonian Ball, held on 16th May at the Grosvenor House Hotel. A month previously, a new biography of the Princess – written by Christopher Warwick, who has admired her for many years – appeared very much as the Princess' own account of some of the controversies of her eventful and sometimes stormy life.

Prince Charles won a medal; h
team Maple Leaf won a cup (b
left); but the Princess of Wales
won everybody's attention with
her casual, stylish pedal-
pushers, when she arrived at
Smith's Lawn on 25th May. W
sunglasses perched on her blo
away hair, she looked thoroug
relaxed, watching her husban
team beat Saracens.

The Queen had, perhaps, less to smile about at the Epsom Derby on 1st June (following pages). Her colt Special Leave had been withdrawn after an indifferent trials performance, and victory passed to the hands of others. But the presence of Prince Philip, Princess Anne, the Queen Mother and the Duke and Duchess of Gloucester made it a relaxing family event.

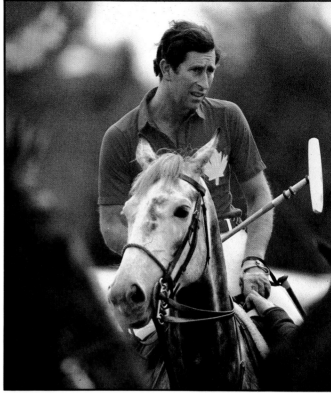

Towards the end of April it was announced that the Queen had appointed three more Knights of the Most Noble Order of the Garter. These were the Duke of Norfolk, hereditary Earl Marshal of England, Admiral of the Fleet Lord Lewin and Lord Richardson of Duntisbourne. On 13th June, the Throne Room at Windsor Castle was filled with almost the entire complement of Knights as the new boys were installed at the annual chapter. After the customary lunch, the service of the Order was held in St George's Chapel, the Queen, Prince Philip, the Prince of Wales and the Queen Mother bringing up the rear of the impressive, slow-moving procession (overleaf).

The Royal Family was out in force again for the four days of Royal Ascot (following pages) from 14th to 17th June, bringing a touch of level-headedness to a meeting frenzied with preoccupation about hairstyles and dress lengths. The big fad this year was the coiffing of hair into effective hats – one head of long hair was teased up and lacquered to form a top hat; another was ranged radially to form a Japanese parasol. Mrs Gertrude Shilling caught the Queen's eye – but necessarily very fleetingly – with a messy turmoil of Union Jacks bearing the motto "Buy British" while a woman designer, Besant by name, created a hat comprising nothing but mirrors, explaining that "when the sun comes out it sparkles."

The nearest any member of the Royal Family got to extravagant hats was the cartwheel-brimmed one which the Duchess of Gloucester wore on the first day. For the rest, it was noticed that the absent Princess of Wales' predilection for feathers had taken the Queen's fancy, and that pill-boxes were popular with Princess Anne as well. Pleasant though it was, the occasion may not prove particularly memorable for the Queen. She had not a single winner in the entire four-day programme, and the BBC's live broadcasting blackout deprived her of a television commentary in the royal box. The Queen even asked the BBC's racing correspondent whether he couldn't do his commentary on Ascot's closed circuit TV instead. "That was nice of her," he beamed.

If 1981 was celebrated for a spectacular Royal Wedding, 1982 for the birth of a future King, then 1983 became renowned above all for a programme of Commonwealth tours for the Prince and Princess of Wales, whose popularity in Australia, New Zealand and Canada exceeded all expectations. The tours themselves were tailor-made to emphasise the importance of youth, as shown by the young, informal trends set by the Princess, and by the unceasing contact both she and Prince Charles had with children. Prince William's presence in Australasia was an added source of excitement. After the uncertainty as to whether he would accompany his parents, it was a delight to see him being brought downs the steps of the aircraft when it landed in Alice Springs at eight o'clock

on the hot Sunday morning of 20th March. An effusive welcome awaited the royal couple the next day at the School of the Air (opposite page). This education-by-wireless service gives daily schooling to children living in the remote parts of the Northern Territory, and the Prince and Princess broadcast to them, answering their questions about Prince William's favourite toys and the number of rooms in Buckingham Palace.

The Australasian triumph caused everyone to expect an anti-climax in Canada. But the Canadians gave the royal couple an unforgettable welcome at Halifax on 14th June. The Princess responded with her special brand of informality, and clothes matching the Maple Leaf flag. (Opposite) At a naval dockyard the next day.

Premier Pierre Trudeau seemed to fall in love with the Princess when he spoke at a banquet she and Prince Charles attended (previous pages) on 15th June. She was an instant success with the children too, shaking hands with hundreds of them at Rothesay two days later (this page). And those who kept an eye on her wardrobe admired her bold, flamenco-style clothes at Shelburne and Bridgewater on 16th June.

The Premier of New Brunswick
followed Mr Trudeau in his
admiration of the Prince and
Princess of Wales, speaking
handsomely of the "triumph of
love" at a State banquet on
14th June (left). Two days
later, the population of St
Andrews cheered them out of the
mists as they arrived for
Sunday morning service (this
page and overleaf). The
previous day they had been
among the Micmac Indians, who
had given the Princess (see
page 307) a Red Indian outfit
for Prince William.

Ottawa blazed in an 80° heat to give the Prince and Princess a formal welcome on Parliament Hill on 20th June (this page) and again at a banquet at Rideau Hall that evening.

The royal couple enjoyed a break from the Maritime Provinces' mists during a relaxing visit to the Ottawa Police Headquarters on 21st June. In Newfoundland, they attended an open-air

reception, where the Princess was a little embarrassed when she had to join in the singing of sea songs at St John's on 23rd June. But she and her husband enjoyed the endless festivities on St John's Day (opposite page) and a chat with the residents of Carbonear the day after (this page).

Klondike fashions dominated
barbecue at Edmonton, and
Prince and Princess (right)
entered into the fun of the
occasion. A more formal, but
equally colourful farewell
dinner the next day (this page)
brought their second
Commonwealth tour to a fitting
end.

Mid-1983 was a particularly happy time for Prince and Princess Michael of Kent as they emerged from Westminster Cathedral at the end of July (left and below), their five-year-old marriage finally recognised and blessed by the Roman Catholic Church. The Prince and Princess attend Anglican and Catholic church services on alternate Sundays. The Queen was all smiles, too, when opening the Royal Society of Edinburgh's premises (below left), and holding a garden party at Holyroodhouse (right) on 29th June. The following day, she reviewed the Royal Scots Regiment there (opposite, below), with Princess Anne (bottom left). The Princess attended many of the regiment's celebrations in this, its 350th year, including an anniversary ball at Edinburgh's Assembly Rooms (below, far left).

nce Andrew's visit to
wport, Rhode Island in mid-
, in support of Britain's
erica's Cup challenge,
an with a reception at the
Colony House. Smiles hid
concern as IRA protestors
kled his arrival. The
kle of a gun salute made
and his detective jump,
re both realised their
ake and were convulsed
relieved laughter. The
ce was in Rhode Island as
t of Peter de Savary,
se efforts to secure the
erica's Cup for Britain
expensive, unsparing
in the unhappy event,
ccessful. The Cup went to
ralia, though all that
ened long after Prince
ew had enjoyed an active
exciting trip.

as only to be expected of
an about to embark on his
year in the Royal Navy
Prince Andrew found him-
thoroughly at home on
motor launch *Lisanola,*
which he saw Britain's

Victory '83 being put through her paces during one of many practice runs. He had the good fortune to be invited aboard the yacht, and tried his hand at sailing her.

ning the traditional
ts of August's Cowes
, Prince Philip looked
d and in good humour,
g *Yeoman XXI* (left),
tching a moment's
t conversation with his
cousin and crew member,
King Constantine of Greece
(top). The King's teenage
daughter, Princess Alexia was
also there (right) as was
Prince Edward, who attended
both as learner (above) and
as competitor.

If the Queen Mother's birthday doesn't quite have the status which offers her daughter the full ceremonial of Trooping the Colour, it is nevertheless an established part of the summer season. Even its ritual is becoming familiar: the assembly of a crowd of hundreds outside the doors of Clarence House, and the chorus of cheers and applause as a large-brimmed hat, bobbing into sight on an upper terrace, eventually reveals a beaming birthday girl (right), bright as a button, proud as Punch, half amused, half moved by the admiring audience below. The odd toddler (bottom picture) hogs the attention for a while – a small distraction compared with what follows

when the Queen Mother comes down to greet her well-wishers. In a reassuring breach of the generation gap, the braver children storm an unobtrusive police guard, and the luckier or more persistent ones reach their royal target with a volley of flowers, cards and chocolates (left, below left). The less fortunate (bottom) find the London bobby a willing intermediary. On this pleasant August morning, the crowds were rewarded by the sight of the Queen Mother's two daughters (below) and the Prince and Princess of Wales enjoying this informal atmosphere before the celebrant's final wave (right).

After a fortnight spent going separate ways, there was a royal reunion on 14th August, when the Queen led her family off *Britannia*'s barge to meet the Queen Mother at Scrabster. Prince Andrew sported a new and, in events, brief beard, while Princess Anne, on the eve of her 33rd birthday, carried her 2½-

year-old daughter Zara ashore (right). The Queen Mother had travelled from the Castle of Mey, where the previous day she had attended a local horticultural show (left). The family came together again for the Braemar Games (above) early in September. As usual, the Prince and Princess of Wales, Princess Alexandra and Mr Angus Ogilvy joined the royal party.

Prince Charles, Princess Diana and Prince William made their own way to their Balmoral holiday, but even royal vacations are fragmented, and both the Prince and Princess undertook several official engagements from the Castle that summer. Princess Diana's brief, private visit to London fired new speculation, which took two months to subside, that she was pregnant, while 14-month-old Prince William contributed to the family's holiday excitement by escaping his nanny's attention and setting off the security alarms. Detectives within the Castle, and police squads without, were quick to react, if rather slower to appreciate the funny side.

te the family upheaval
ing Princess Margaret's
tion and divorce, Lord
on's relationship with
children remained firm
ordial. Witness the
n October 1983, when
Viscount Linley and Lady
Sarah Armstrong-Jones were at
a Foyle's literary luncheon
in London to help their
father and stepmother (above)
launch Lord Snowdon's new
photographic book, *Sittings*.

Queen was one of four
rents at the Bayswater
m on 20th October of
ss Theodora, fourth
of King Constantine of
. His wife, Queen Anne-
was joined by her
Queen Margrethe of
Denmark (in mauve), while
sister-in-law Queen Sofia of
Spain brought two of her
children, Cristina and Felipe
(top right). Prince Paul,
Prince Nicholas and Princess
Alexia of Greece (opposite,
top) also attended.

Memories dominated early November. On the 2nd, the Queen unveiled Lord Mountbatten's statue at Horse Guards (top) before almost all the Royal Family (above, far left). The following week, the Queen Mother (opposite) again visited the Field of Remembrance at Westminster, and joined many relatives at the Cenotaph on Remembrance Day. On this occasion it was Prince Charles who laid the first wreath, rather than the Queen, who was then in Kenya.

Kenya's Remembrance Day was observed on the original Armistice anniversary, 11th November, and the Queen and Prince Philip led Kenya's and the Commonwealth's tribute in a quiet, solemn ceremony in Nairobi. Her cluster of poppies and the black of her gloves, shoes and patterned dress offered the only similarities to the sombre garb of a Whitehall ceremony: Prince Philip's tropical rig looked strangely incongruous. This was not the only wreath the Queen laid that day: early in the morning she had placed a tribute of white lilies on the tomb of Jomo Kenyatta, the former President who had led his country to independence in 1963.

Buffalo at close range
(right) failed to deter the
Queen as, with marksman
Richard Prickett (above) she
toured the Treetops water
hole where, almost 32 years
before, she succeeded to the
Throne. Both the Queen and
the Prince seemed bemused by
the drastic changes they saw.

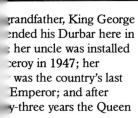

grandfather, King George
ended his Durbar here in
; her uncle was installed
ceroy in 1947; her
was the country's last
Emperor; and after
y-three years the Queen
herself was back in Delhi. In
1961 she had been greeted by
President Nehru. Now his
daughter, Mrs Indira Gandhi
welcomed Her Majesty, who
looked delighted to be
visiting India again.

The massive, Lutyens-design
Hyderabad House, with its
reminders of the British Raj,
was the setting for some
informal talks between the
Queen and Mrs Ghandi, whie
were filmed for inclusion in
the Queen's Christmas messa
a month later.

The Queen visited the fabled Red Fort in Delhi (left) and Mahatma Gandhi's tomb at Rajghat. Here she wore, in place of her own shoes, airline 'slipperettes'. (Above and right) a pre-lunch photo-call with Mrs Gandhi at Hyderabad House. (Opposite, below) the Queen presenting the Order of Merit to Mother Theresa in Delhi the following day.

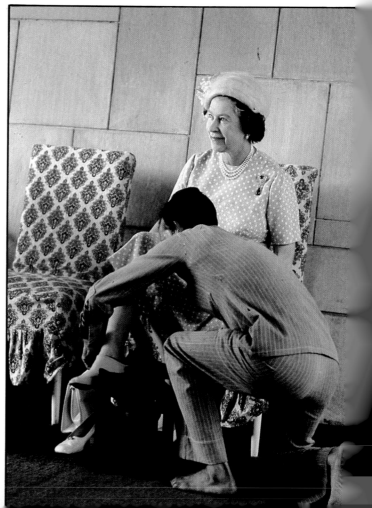

...ight of the Queen's
...d day in India was her
...f St Thomas' School.
...ed by girls with incense
...above), she visited
...imary department
...and then hopped into
...nquin carried by senior
...dressed as male
...s – who performed a
...lled *The Awakening of
Womanhood*.

(Previous pages) the Princess of Wales at Wantage on 2nd December (right) and visiting victims of the Harrods bomb explosion on the 19th. The approach of Prince William's second Christmas was marked by a photo session in the garden of his parents' London home, Kensington Palace.

Crown-Princess Marie-Aglae of Liechtenstein (left) accompanied the Prince and Princess of Wales on the Alpine slopes at the start of their skiing holiday on 8th January, 1984. The early bargain struck between Prince

and Press was honoured and the royal couple eventually soared to the top of Hoch Eck (right and bottom) to begin a much appreciated private vacation.

succession of royal gala
...nings brightened a gloomy
...ish winter. On 23rd
...ruary, the Queen Mother
...nded the Elgar commemor-
...e concert at Westminster
...ey (far left). She was at
...Odeon, Leicester Square,
...he premiere of *Champions*
...t days later (left), with
...cess Anne (opposite, top
...re). The Queen also
...ed the Odeon (opposite,
...eft) to see *The Dresser*
...9th March. On 12th April,
...Duchess of Kent attended
...Amir of Bahrain's State
...uet in London (opposite,
...ight), while a month
...er, Prince and Princess
...ael (this page) had
...ded a London Coliseum
...rmance of the opera
...na. The Princess exuded
...pecial combination of
...ty and informal charm
...as earned her the
...iption "More royal than
...yals".

The Queen and Prince Philip left London on 23rd March for a five-day State Visit to Jordan. Controversial for its political and security implications, the tour began cautiously, with a stop-over in Cyprus and a circuitous route avoiding Syria. But it was all smiles when the royal couple finally arrived (these pages) in Amman to be greeted by King Hussein, whose

sometimes precarious political relations with the West have never shaken his personal friendship with the British Royal Family. His regard for the Queen and Prince Philip was reflected in the resplendent banquet he and Queen Noor (far left) gave that first evening – a full State occasion, with every royal utterance scrupulously combed for political undertones. The Queen praised King Hussein's unceasing attempts to find a solution to the Palestinian problem, while the King addressed his country's cause to the 'sense of justice of the British people. We appreciate their courageous views and keenness to eliminate the mistakes of the past.'

Everything and everyone was dwarfed by the dimensions of Petra, the ancient trading centre built by the Nabateans two thousand years ago. The Queen and Prince Philip, accompanied as they were almost everywhere on this tour by Hussein and his Queen, walked into the ruined city to capture the grandeur of its approaches.

was heavily guarded
...e) and cleared of most of
...e-dwelling families,
...h some inhabitants –
...ing this New Zealand-
...mother (top) – were
...ted to the Queen. This
...r last sightseeing
...of the tour, and the
...ouple stayed at King
...n's palace at Aqaba
...ght, leaving (left)
...ay.

...ess Diana admitted the ...s of morning sickness ...cester in March ...e), but at Stanmore the ...ay (right), seemed in ...spirits. With the ...ach of Easter, no end of presents were being offered her – a knitted doll for her baby at Glastonbury (top right) and Easter eggs for Prince William at Stoke (left).

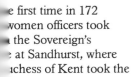

e first time in 172
women officers took
the Sovereign's
e at Sandhurst, where
chess of Kent took the
Salute on 6th April. Just
after the Queen's Jordanian
visit, Queen Noor (above
right) saw her nephew receive
his commission.

the Duke of Beaufort's
only two months before,
ainton Horse Trials in
inevitably lacked its
festive air. But the
n was there (far right),
aptain Mark Phillips
competed, though
cessfully, while his
en Peter (right) and
above) looked as
ievous as ever, and
ed the public with some
aining distractions.

Spring flowers for the Princess of Wales as she arrived at Wellington College at Crowthorne on 16th April, to hear the National Children's Orchestra in rehearsal. Though she is patron of the orchestra, she admitted that music was not her strong point at school. Prince William might do better, however, as his mother was presented with a quarter-size violin to take back for him. Next day, Princess Alexandra was presenting radio and television awards in London – to the delight of the BBC who bagged most of them. Jan Leeming, Frank Bough and David Coleman (opposite page) were proud recipients, while ITV's George Cole and Dennis Waterman (bottom left) made the most of their moment of glory.

Queen discharged her ... al Maundy obligations ... ear at one of the most ... tive of small English ... drals, when she distributed purses of specially-minted money to 58 men and 58 women at Southwell Minster, near Newark, on 19th April. Then she and Prince

Philip met ice-dancing royalty when Olympic champions Jayne Torvill and Christopher Dean were presented at a Nottingham Council reception. After the enormous surge of patriotism and pride which surrounded the young couple as they easily secured their gold medal at Sarajevo – an achievement watched by Princess Anne and on which the Queen personally telegraphed her congratulations – this was a most popular royal event.

Seemingly incapable of radiating anything but the joy of being an octogenarian, the doyenne of the Royal Family was as busy as ever on 10th May, 1984. That afternoon, the Queen Mother went to All Saints Church at Ascot to open its new church hall (these pages). She has no particular connection with the church, but that didn't stop her from enjoying a pleasantly informal afternoon, brightened by the singing of its forty-strong choir. Of course, they asked her to pose for a photograph, and the Queen Mother oblige as she always does. And as she's also good at planting trees, she did that too.

...lection of Prince
...les' early season polo
...hes. (Above) playing at
...dsor on 13th May for
...enya against Downey
...'s in the final of the
...ey Moore Cup: Ingwenya
...4-2. (Left and top right)
...e same day, playing for
...dsor against Travelwise:
...sor lost 9-6½.
...osite page, top left and
...ght) playing at Windsor
...th May for Rajasthan
...Club against Laurent
...r. The Queen saw his
...lose 7-3. (Right and far
...laying at Windsor on
...May for Les Diables
... beating Chopendoz 8-7
...t of the Princess of
... (Far right, and
...ite, top centre) in the
...r finals of the Queen's
...t Windsor on 3rd June,
...his team, Les Diables
... beat Piaget 10-7.

By most accounts the Royal Windsor Horse Show lacked touch of extravagance usual associated with this prestigious annual event, but any occasion staged at Home Park, Windsor, within sight of the Queen's Berkshire home, and graced by royalty determined to enjoy their day's leisure, cannot be mediocre for long. So even the threat of indifferent weather could not put off the many spectators as the Queen sported her most comfortable functional country clothes to tramp the ground where Prince Philip would be competing during the four-day event. As is often the case, the Duke's only surviving sister, Princess Sophie of Hanover (bottom left) belied her 70 years to brave a cold, breezy day in support of her brother, whose two-fold aim was to regain the Harrods International Driving Grand

Prix which he lost last year, and win a place in the British team for the World Driving Championships in Hungary in August. Princess Anne (above), Prince Edward and Prince Paul of Greece (top picture) were there to see Prince Philip take the lead after the first day's presentation and dressage (opposite page), despite a strict line taken by the judges, and a heart stopping

moment when his two leading horses suddenly took a dislike to each other. Prince Philip, who had suffered a number of spills earlier in the season when driving novice horses, seemed much more confident after his near victory the previous week at a Brighton carriage-driving event (in which Prince Michael also competed), and was in any case back with his familiar team of Cleveland bays/Oldenburg crosses, owned by the Queen. These days, it seems, no major equestrian event escapes the presence of Princess Anne's two children, and sure enough, Master Peter Phillips looked engrossed with the proceedings as, supervised by the Queen (opposite page), he put his pair of miniature binoculars to good use. But his quiet

behaviour didn't last and, before long, he was being firmly taken in hand by Princess Anne (above). Sister Zara seemed much more amenable, possibly because she was looking forward to her 3rd birthday for which, four days later, she would throw a small party for her young friends and relations. There was also an unexpected treat at Windsor when Prince Philip allowed both Peter and Zara to ride in his driving carriage. Typically, it was Peter who took the whip, and commanded the horses, while Zara had to be reassured by her mother. Meanwhile, Prince

Philip had two more stages to complete, and unfortunately he was to lose ground. Going for total accuracy in the marathon lost him precious time points, and he was not helped by a broken carriage cable after colliding with a branch just before the obstacle section. In the final analysis, he had dropped to seventh place, and the Queen found herself once again congratulating Tjeerd Velstra, last year's winner, on retaining the championship. But she could afford a smile (top, with King Constantine): her own private carriage won a coaching event, and Prince Philip still secured his passage to Hungary.

The Princess of Wales looking
proudly pregnant (above) as
she awaited her car after a
banquet given by the
President of the Royal
Society of Arts, Sir Hugh
Casson, (right) in Piccadilly
on 14th May. Back in
September, both the Princess
and Sir Hugh had submitted
their own portrait sketches
of Prince William and Prince
Charles respectively for a
publication in aid of Mencap.
The Princess wore white
again, but this time with
gold sequins, for the Royal
Opera House Development
Appeal concert six days later
(top right and opposite).

...oyals can resist
...g the Chelsea Flower
..., held this year on 21st
... The Queen (above and
...site, top left) attended
... Princess Margaret (right
... left), another
... visitor; the Duchess
...oucester (above)
...panied Princess Alice;
...rincess Michael (left)

...ave picked up a few tips
...r new rose garden at
...r Lyppiatt. Royal
...ds included Prince
...s, who took Princess
...along, and Prince
...l, though Prince Philip
...cry off at the last
...t to attend World
...e Fund meetings in
...gton.

ss Michael looked every
e Edwardian beauty in
ic, figure-hugging
g robe, and a choker
would have made even
Alexandra a trifle
s. With Prince Michael,

she was attending a gala
performance at the London
Coliseum on 22nd May of
Onegin, by the late John
Cranko, chosen by the London
Festival Ballet to open its
1984 season.

(Top, and opposite page) a colourfully-dressed Princess Alexandra visiting Cranleigh School in Surrey on 23rd May, while on the same day the Princess of Wales was making her second visit to the Albany Trust in Deptford (left). She had to run the gauntlet of several political controversies, including a plea to help prevent the possible abolition of the GLC. She said she would speak to her father, before a crucial vote in the House of Lords. Two of Princess Anne's many engagements in May took her to RAF Lyneham (top left) on the 3rd, and to the Surrey County Show at Guildford on the 28th (above, left). But it was a quiet month for Princess Michael, seen (above) competing at the Amberley Horse Trials on 5th May.

The high-goal polo season brought Prince Charles to Windsor on 24th May. His team won 8-7, to the delight of Princess Diana, who now really seems to enjoy polo.

Queen Mother began a
e-day tour of the Channel
ds on 30th May. First
of call was Guernsey,
h 'holds many happy
ories for me, renewed
ugh the living bonds
h continue to link
rnsey and the Crown.' As
ywhere in the islands,
Queen Mother, who first
ed them with King George
the aftermath of
ation exactly thirty-
years before, was a
lar guest, and nowhere
so than on Sark, where
enteel way of island
emed tailor-made for
Queen Mother's very
idual style of carrying
er duties. She forsook
elicopter in which she
rrived (left) for a
and carriage (above),

...e traditional means of
...ouring the island. That
...vening, the Royal Yacht
...ritannia, in which she had
...iled to Guernsey, took her
... Jersey, where she landed
...e next morning (far right).
...s on previous days, her
...ıgagement book was packed,
...t she smiled and chatted
...r way through the
...ceptions, visits and those
...ıannel Island specialities,
...e *vins d'honneur.* The Queen
...other has been known in
...ars past to try her hand at
...ooker or billiards. When
...e visited the Maufant Youth
...ntre in Jersey, she
...duated to the pool table
...ft), slamming in a ball to
... delight of her hosts who
...d tactfully placed it where
... could hardly miss! Such
...ne prerogative of Queens,
...ndeed a tour such as this
...ıe prerogative of their
...ojects. Normally, at this
...e of year, the Queen

Mother does a round trip taking in the Cinque Ports, of which she is Lord Warden. But, with the D-Day anniversary close by, nothing could have been more appropriate as this all too rare return to what Churchill called 'our dear Channel Islands.'

A sixty-eight-man parachute drop (opposite, top) by soldiers who had fought in the Falklands provided a spectacular start to Prince Charles' visit on 5th June to Ranville in Normandy to commemorate D-Day with the Parachute Regiment. It was a day of pride for the veterans who marched past their Colonel-in-Chief (top) and of gratitude for the Prince, who laid a wreath where 2,500 servicemen lie buried in the town's military cemetery (above).

(Left) the Princess of Wales attended the premiere of *Indiana Jones and the Temple of Doom*, in Leicester Square on 11th June. Next day Prince William posed – though over a week early – for a photocall at Kensington Palace in celebration of his second birthday, 21st June. Mother, child and family came together again – on the parade ground (above) and on the Palace balcony (following pages) for Trooping the Colour on 16th June.

The Princess of Wales took delivery of a new Ford Escort convertible late in Spring, and drove it to Cirencester on 28th June to watch Prince Charles play in the Warwickshire Cup. His team won, though narrowly, while his wife attracted the interest of spectators by her bright blue culottes and her healthy tan. It was only three days to her 23rd birthday, which she spent at yet another polo match, and which was celebrated by many tributes to the enormous contribution she had made in three years to the popularity of the monarchy.

"Two months later than planned, but better late than never!" September 24th, 1984 at last saw the Queen and Prince Philip in Canada for the fifteenth time. On this occasion the welcoming province was New Brunswick, high on bicentennial celebrations, and Moncton received the royal visitors. The ceremony of welcome followed a familiar pattern, but the unofficial antics of youngsters (above and right) lent a delightful unpredictability to it all. Julie McLean was there officially (opposite), and presented her bouquet beautifully.

Shediac's celebrated lobsters were out of season, so the townsfolk treated the Queen to some local entertainment instead (left). At 102, Mrs Leonie Williams (top left) offered the Queen's bou[quet], an honour usually reser[ved for] children. Then it was ba[ck to] Moncton for an open-air reception at Victoria Par[k] (above).

Sunshine greeted the next d
too, and leafy, loyalist
Fredericton looked its pristi
sparkling best. The clash of
bells drifting over its elegan
streets called the faithful to
prayer at Christ Church
Cathedral, where two very
special worshippers would
head the congregation.
Archbishop Nutter (far left)
the honours and, only ten d
from the event, could not re
a congratulatory word to th
Queen on the birth of Princ
Harry. "I may say as a
grandparent — and we hav
many grandparents in this
congregation — how much
rejoice," he enthused. Ther
was no whisper of dissent
the entire town — a remin
that loyalty and devotion to
Crown and those who
represent it is almost a way
life here.

Princess Anne once said h
difficult it is to take an
intelligent interest in thing
and still wear a grin. The
Queen's studious apprecia
of an hour of local songs I
her looking somewhat
absorbed (left), though she
pleased by the display of
cultural togetherness whic
English, Acadian and Ind
elements of the programr
offered. Prince Philip (far
took a more relaxed attitu
engaging her in some
light-hearted banter (top)
making great play of one
Loyalist girl's spontaneou
attention to her sovereig
(right). Those with a sen:
history — the Queen is
certainly one — will relis
thought that the bandsh
which she sat has surviv
full 124 years since the P
was opened by the Princ
Wales in 1860.

The Hotel Beauséjour was th[e] Queen's home during her two-day stay at Moncton, but also became a venue of State when, at the end of her secon[d] day, she and Prince Philip attended a banquet given by New Brunswick's Premier, Richard Hatfield. The Quee[n] resplendent in her gorgeous family jewels and wearing th[e] Sovereign's insignia of the Order of Canada, made no secret of her pleasure at bei[ng] back. "This is an historic ye[ar] for New Brunswick," she sa[id] "and you have indeed a lot [to] celebrate." And she praised [the] successive descendants of American Loyalists, Acadian[s] Irish, Scots and Europeans [in] accepting the challenges of coexistence.

Ottawa rarely fails her Queen, and the military display greeting her in the national capital was a model of panache and precision. The Queen's contribution to the blaze of colour was her bright scarlet coat, which matched the uniforms around her, the red carpet on which she walked, and the striped awning under which she replied to the Prime Minister's speech of welcome.

The royal barge (previous page) took the Queen and Prince Philip from Morrisburg's Crysler Park Marina to the Royal Yacht — their home for the next stage of the tour. The following day was a big one for Minh Duc Nguyen, eager to show off her beautiful posy (bottom left)– before presenting it to the Queen at Trinity Church, Cornwall. Canon Peever (opposite) took the royal couple on a tour of the church.

g Sarah Eisen stole the
when she misbehaved
to the Queen's arrival in
nia (right) at Toronto,
resented her bouquet
he sweetest of smiles
site). "We make very

great demands of you,"
Ontario's Premier told the
Queen at the Legislative
Building. "It's a very real
pleasure," she reassured him
(above).

The Six Nations is one of Canada's largest Indian reserves, and it was there that the Queen and Prince Philip travelled by car after landing in mid-afternoon at Brantfo Airport. Chief Wellingto Staats was the first to gr them, acting as host and throughout the thirty-mi

visit. The 10,000 spectators found the Queen relaxed and chatty as she strolled under the pine trees, despite a chilly wind and threatening skies. She dedicated as a National Historic Site the expensively-restored Mohawk Chapel, which provided the backdrop t... the ceremony of welcome... planted her own silver p... the chapel grounds.

The Six Nations' fierce guardianship of their trac... and culture is just the ki... thing the Queen admires...

virtue in itself, and a colourful contribution to the Canadian character. She will also have been gratified by the many royal associations boasted by the chapel: the land on which it stands was granted by George III, who also gifted the solid oak coat of arms and the wooden tablets engraved with the Apostles' Creed, Lord's Prayer and Ten Commandments; Queen Anne had sent out a set of Communion silver seventy years earlier; Edward VII granted it royal status in 1904 and one of the stained glass windows now bears the present Queen's cypher. Her visit emphasised the Mohawk long relationship with the Crown, and Chief Staats asked her specifically "to continue the tradition of watchfulness over the people of the Six Nations

From the Cenotaph, the Queen took a leisurely walk to Nathan Phillips Square, stopping to chat with schoolchildren along the way (top right). One of them was pleasantly surprised to find she wasn't "a snob", while another, wearing tiara and makeshift robe, discussed her ambition to be Queen one day. The real Queen may have been surprised at Toronto's changing appearance and paid tribute to it as "a city which has reason to be proud of what has been achieved in 150 years." One such recent achievement is the Convention Centre which she visited that afternoon, taking the escalator ride (right) very much in her stride.

Prince Philip left the Canadian tour at Sudbury, and the Queen continued the final stage on her own. It took her to Manitoba which, as its Premier was quick to point out, she had last visited all of fourteen years ago. The reminder came at a Provincial Governement dinner, and was reinforced by the Premier's gift of a book of previous royal visits to the province. "I look forward," the Queen responded, "to finding in this volume the threads which my family have contributed to the tapestry of Manitoba's history."

Two of the Queen's more cultural engagements of day — her last full day in Canada — took her to the Costume Museum at Du for the parade of historic fashions (far left), and to Boniface site, in one of Winnipeg's suburbs, whe Voyageurs of the Red Ri Brigade re-enacted the ar (left) of La Vérendrye at Maurepas, near Selkirk, 2 years ago. The Queen's g on her subsequent walk through La Vérendrye Pa (opposite) was Mr Justice Michel Monnin (bottom picture), authentically dr as one of La Vérendrye's

Prime Minister Mulroney greeted the Queen for the [first] time at the Canadian Government's farewell di[nner] at the Winnipeg Conventi[on] Centre — having himself arrived with his popular [wife] Mila, a few minutes earlie[r. "I] am saddened at the task [of] bidding you farewell," he [said.] "You and Prince Philip ha[ve] been models of gracious understanding, sympathe[tic] and symbolic of our histo[ric] evolution." The complime[nt] earned a stalwart respons[e] from the Queen: "I shall continue to fulfil my dutie[s as] Queen of Canada to the be[st of] my abilities and in the inte[rest] of all Canadians."

doubtedly the most sensational
line from Diana's 1985
drobe is this stunning outfit
ich she wore at a banquet given
the Mayor of Florence. The low
st is a particularly favourite
racteristic, but the rich, black
et bodice with its sparkling
ern of royal blue stars and
gles had fashion pundits
ching for superlatives.
igner Jacques Azagury became
lebrity overnight. Daytime
ance came from Victor
lstein, with (overleaf) a
isticated, wine-coloured silk
s finely striped with white.
contrast between the tight,
cummerbund belt and the
er bow and sleeves offered a
nce well complemented by the
, matching saucer hat.

Re-cycling has been Diana's fashion hallmark. She had worn this pink ensemble back in 1983, but the Sicilians saw it again, subtly varied, and enhanced by the matching hat with its upturned brim.

Another of Diana's favourites is this striking red suit – a Spanish bullfighter style zoot suit, as it became dubbed in Canada in 1983. Here, Diana wears it for a tour of the Renaissance quarter of Florence, with the subtle addition of a polka-dot blouse underneath. The long lapels and low, straight jacket didn't appeal overmuch to the Italians. "Too much," said one of their fashion experts; "a little provincial." Nevertheless, it was certainly an outfit to catch the eye, and it is doubtful if Diana was too discouraged. Jasper Conran, the suit's designer, would be hard to replace. (Overleaf) the Princess draped in black for her Vatican audience; and more casually dressed for a visit to Milan's churches.

There was a strange irony about Diana's choice of clothes for Thursday, 2nd May, 1985. On what proved to be the sunniest day of the Italian tour with Prince Charles, she was wearing a dress-ensemble overflowing with clouds. The scene was the little port of Trani, one of the prettiest towns in the whole of their 17-day visit, alive with festive decorations and the warmest of welcomes. They

made a leisurely tour of the 11th-century cathedral, during which fleeting royal appearances in doorways and on parapets were greeted with shouts of "Regina, regina" – a sure sign that, for the ebullient and appreciative Italians at least, Diana was already their queen. (Over) the Princess visited the port of La Spezia after a late decision to join Prince Charles who was to have toured the port alone.

Italians' send-off was a
y affair. Charles and
's two young children
pined the Yacht at
e, and the foursome
ured on her deck – Harry
much grown; William slimmer
– to wave farewell. These
final pictures followed the
colourful scenes (overleaf)
as the royal couple toured
the waterways of Venice.

There was enormous interest in the Prince and Princess of Wales' four-day trip to America late in 1985. Short though it was, it reflected their official lifestyle perfectly: contacts with the Reagans (opposite, bottom left) and the more dependant (bottom); moments of solemnity (left, right) and of recreation (below); and glimpses of Diana in settings formal (far left) and informal (opposite, bottom right).

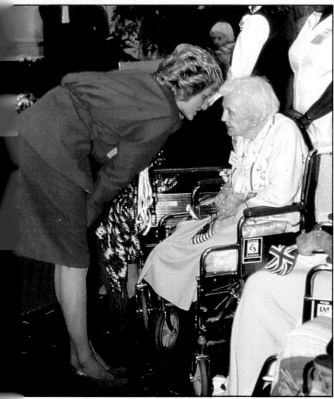

The tour was full of highlights and with never a dull moment. The elation a polo victory for the Prince (opposite, top left) at Palm Beach contrasted with the poignancy of the terminally ill Jonathan Lollar, whose wish to give Diana a copy of his record (above left) was granted. The chumminess between Princess and First Lady (opposite, top right) proved that the greetings on the night of the White House banquet (far right) were genuinely warm. And the sumptuous display of British goods at J C Penne (right) came second only that famous gala at Palm Beach's Breakers Hotel (above). As Prince and Princess waved farewell (left) it seemed evident that the future of the monarchy – popular both home and abroad – was i safe hands.

JACKIE STEWART
CELEBRITY CHALLENGE

THE TEAM

Sarah and Andrew are connoisseurs of the [...] world, and the public had its first [oppor]tunity to see them in a relaxed setting at the [...] Show. It was hardly the most glamorous of [occas]ions, with the royal couple and the Queen [all w]rapped up in woollies and wellies against a [...] damp and unseasonal May afternoon.

(Previous pages) a kiss from Andrew on her engagement day; a glimps
of the royal ruby-and-diamond engagement ring; and a huge bow
ribbon for one of Sarah's first official outings with Andrew. (These
pages) High fashion at Ascot: Sarah with Princess Margaret (top),
Princess Anne (above) and (opposite page) the Queen Mother and
Princess Michael.

...arly one of the family: Sarah appears (top) for the second time on the ...ace balcony, after the Queen's birthday parade (left and overleaf) in ...e, along with seasoned royals like the Queen Mother (right), Princess ...ana and Princess Michael of Kent (above).

(Previous page) All smiles for Sarah and Andrew during a visit to Northern Ireland in June. (These pages). Andrew looks on proudly as Sarah presents the Queen's Cup to Prince Charles' victorious polo team that month. (Overleaf) Sarah sporting some of her more complicated millinery at a friend's summer wedding in London.

*London was a patriot's delight on the wedding day, with
impromptu demonstrations of loyalty all along the route before
the groom and his brother emerged into public view.*

A momentary change in the weather as the royal carriages arrive at Sanctuary Green. Though it stayed favourable, the occasional black cloud kept crowds alert for the odd shower. Meanwhile an airship bearing a "Good Luck" message hovered above Parliament (left).

Crowds caught just a glimpse of Sarah's top-secret wedding dress as she rode in the Glass Coach with her father. (Following pages) a smiling Queen and Prince Philip arrive for the service.

When her carriage stopped at the Abbey (above) Sarah was 20 minutes away from becoming Duchess of York. Her 17$\frac{1}{2}$-foot-long train gave occasional problems but her progress up the aisle to the Sacrarium (following page) was measured and confident. So was her return, to face in-laws clearly delighted to count her as one of them.

"I'll tell you one thing," Sarah said just before her wedding; "there'll be nothing else like it." She was talking of her wedding dress and she was proved right on the day. Pearl and sequin embroidery and interwoven initials, crests and designs were its hallmarks. No wonder she was smiling (right)!

Royalty and little helpers in waiting before and during the service. (Above right) Ronald Ferguson with bride and groom at the sanctuary rail. (Opposite) the triumphant bridal walk down the aisle.

Like all royal brides before her, Sarah's last duty before she walked from the Sacrarium was to curtsey to the Queen, a manoeuvre achieved (top left) with supreme aplomb and a broad smile! Prince William led the pages and bridesmaids out after her (above), while the camera caught a rare Fergie grimace as she tried to lift her billowing dress and train back into the carriage (right).

The sun shone, briefly, as Sarah and Andrew emerged from beneath the blue awning with its distinctive white-stripe trimming, past a guard of honour formed by forty seamen who had once served on the same ships as the groom. For the first time the public had a full and lingering view of Sarah's magnificent dress.

(Right) Andrew and Sarah walk past their sailor guard to await their carriage (left). Andrew helps (above left) with her long train before (top) she climbs into the coach.

Sarah and Andrew are first out of the Abbey (above right) and quickly away while other members of the Royal Family await their carriages – among them, the Queen, Queen Mother, Prince and Princess of Wales and Princess Anne (above left), and Prince and Princess Michael of Kent with their children, Freddie and Ella (top).

It was a sunny and light-hearted drive back to Buckingham Palace and both Sarah and Andrew enjoyed the heady atmosphere to the full. At the end of their first journey together as man and wife, Sarah's first act was to give each of her bridesmaids and pages a huge kiss — and they couldn't line up fast enough to be on the receiving end.

The happy couple homeward bound (above and left) in pleasant, warm sunshine, followed by the Queen with Major Ferguson (seen, top right, leaving the Abbey) and Prince Philip, in cheerful and animated conversation (right) with Sarah's mother. The crowd lost no time, of course, in taking over the Mall when the carriages had passed.

Prince Edward (top) takes charge of bridesmaids and pages, while the Queen Mother (above) travels in more sedate company. (Opposite) Sarah and Andrew find time for a quick word amid all the cheering.

Triumphal processions follow the bride and groom (above left) back to the Palace. The elder bridesmaids and pages (left) are followed by Prince Philip with Mrs. Susan Barrantes (top & right) mother of the bride, and by the Queen Mother with Princess Margaret and her children.

Two hands raised as one (right) as Andrew and Sarah head for home, via Trafalgar Square and Admiralty Arch (left). Charles and Diana (above) seem more cautious, while the Queen hangs on to her hat (above right) in a stiffish breeze as she drove back with Sarah's father. Top: Princess Anne and her husband in carefree mood.

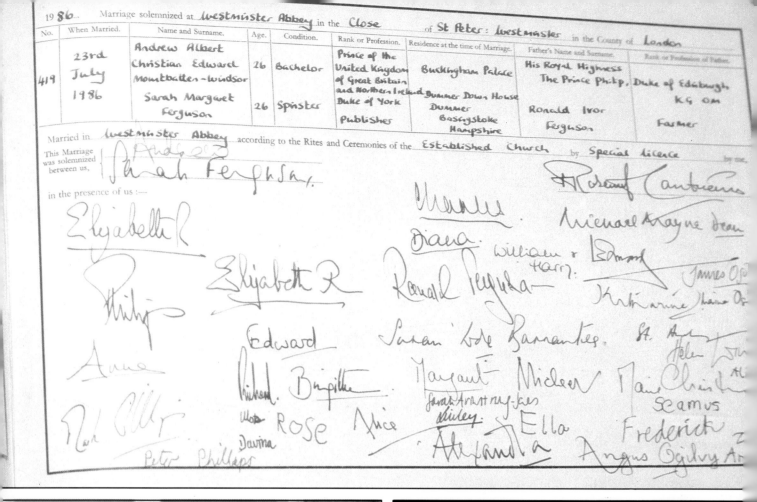

No.	When Married.	Name and Surname.	Age.	Condition.	Rank or Profession.	Residence at the time of Marriage.	Father's Name and Surname.	Rank or Profession of Father.
419	23rd July 1986	Andrew Albert Christian Edward Mountbatten-Windsor	26	Bachelor	Prince of the United Kingdom of Great Britain and Northern Ireland Duke of York	Buckingham Palace	His Royal Highness The Prince Philip	Duke of Edinburgh K G OM
		Sarah Margaret Ferguson	26	Spinster	Publishers	Dummer Down House Dummer Basingstoke Hampshire	Ronald Ivor Ferguson	Farmer

1986. Marriage solemnized at *Westminster Abbey* in the Close of St Peter: *Westminster* in the County of *London*

Married in *Westminster Abbey* according to the Rites and Ceremonies of the *Established Church* by *Special Licence* by me,

This Marriage was solemnized between us,

Andrew
Sarah Ferguson.
Robert Cantuar

in the presence of us :—

Elizabeth R *Charles* *Michael Mayne Dean*
Philip *Elizabeth R* *Diana* *William & Edward* *James Og...*
Anne *Edward* *Ronald Ferguson* *Harry.* *Katharine* ...
Richard. Birgitte *Susan Doe Barrantes.* *St. A...*
Peter Phillips *Davina* *Rose* *Alice* *Margaret Michael* *Marie Christi...*
Sarah Armstrong-Jones *Seamus*
Linley *Ella* *Frederick*
Alexandra *Angus Ogilvy A...*

Everybody in the family put their name on the register (top) though Princess Diana wrote in William's and Harry's for them. And all appeared on the balcony (above and left) from which the novices must have been amazed at the sight of hundreds of thousands surging down the Mall towards them (right).

New faces on the balcony (top) include Major Ferguson, Seamus Makim, Andrew Ferguson, Mrs Barrantes, Lady Rosanagh Innes-Ker, Laura Fellowes — and, of course, the bride. Gallant Prince Andrew gives his wife a helping hand (above) with her train as they go back inside, leaving the crowd to drift away (left).

The Royal Standard (top picture) flying high over Buckingham Palace as the crowds swarm round to see the bride and groom on the balcony. Prince Harry didn't attend the service but (right) was given a good view of the crowds below. For the rest there was a lot of waving and pointing as banners bearing witty messages were raised high.

Previous page: a balcony of royals.
These pages: Sarah and Andrew indulge in a
kiss and a moment's fun with the crowd.
Overleaf: eyes front, 47 times, for the official
photograph.

Members of the Royal Family mingle with chefs, footmen, maids and valets to send the new Duke and Duchess of York off in grand style. The Queen, in particularly good humour, actually ran after the carriage as it moved off with its decorative bunting, drawn by four of her Windsor Greys.

The final ceremony on a day of ceremonies was by royal standards pretty informal. Andrew and Sarah arrived (right) at the Royal Hospital, Chelsea, where the bride received a bouquet (above right). Then it was into the royal red helicopter for an 11–minute flight to London Airport and a well-deserved honeymoon.

The Queen's visit to China heralded six days of vibrant colour,
reflected even in her choice of clothes. She arrived at Peking (below)
wearing imperial yellow, while full-blooded red complimented her
Communist hosts at the welcoming ceremonies in Tien Amen Square.
(Opposite, below) with President Li in the People's Great Hall.

Queen was fascinated by the Forbidden City, a palace complex
000 buildings that once housed the Emperors and their vast
es. Inside the Hall of Supreme Harmony (above and top) she
he centuries-old Dragon Throne; she marvelled at this ornately-
d staircase (left), and walked beside ornamental fishponds in the
rial Gardens.

dent Li's welcoming State Banquet, where the Queen met
one from Foreign Minister Wu Xuegian (top) to a troupe of
ese Theatre Revue performers (left), was a delight. Ornamental
swam in pools inset among the beautifully-decorated place-
gs (above), and mutual toasting (right) seemed not just friendly,
most interminable.

...oyal progress was at times fairly placid, with leisurely lunches
...ve) and streets cleared of sightseers (left), and at times hectic.
...e crowds of officials, tourists and townspeople followed her
...austible trek along the Great Wall (previous pages), and through
...ghai's streets (top) on her way to sample China tea at the Tea-
...e (right).

Over fifteen hundred children swarmed onto the landing area at Shanghai airport to provide what must surely be the Queen's most dazzling welcome ever. That night, she returned the compliment, hosting President Li at a banquet on board Britannia, and a quayside performance of Beating Retreat by the Royal Marines.

热烈欢迎伊丽莎白二世女王陛下和爱丁堡公爵殿下！

WARM WELCOME TO HER MAJESTY QUEEN ELIZABETH II AND HIS ROYAL HIGHNESS THE DUKE OF EDINBURGH!

At Xi'an, the Queen became one of very few visitors to walk among the famous 'terracotta army', commissioned by the first Chin Emperor 2,300 years ago to guard his tomb. Opposite: the Queen with Buddhist monks (top) at a hilltop temple near Kunming, and (below) watched by brightly-dressed children at Kunming's Ethnic Minorities Institute.

It was at Kunming that the Queen enjoyed a brief glimpse of rural China, as she and Prince Philip toured areas (top and left) around the Buddhist temple. They lunched at an island on Lake Dianchi after a relaxing, highly visual trip on a sprucely painted boat (above).

r lunch *(left and above)* on her last full day in China, the
ocence and charm of hundreds of youngsters delighted the
en when she visited the Children's Palace in Canton. They
ormed dances and songs for her – including, appropriately, a well-
ulated version of Auld Lang Syne.

Previous pages: a dragon display·was the last the Queen saw of China, as Britannia took her for her second visit to Hong Kong. With an afternoon at the racecourse as its most colourful event (these pages), the two-day visit must have seemed as close to home as the Queen could have wished for.